Instructor's Manual to Accompany

THE **D Y N A M I C S** *of Social Welfare Policy*

JOEL BLAU *with Mimi Abramovitz*

OXFORD
UNIVERSITY PRESS

2004

OXFORD

UNIVERSITY PRESS

Oxford   New York
Auckland   Bangkok   Buenos Aires   Cape Town   Chennai
Dar es Salaam   Delhi   Hong Kong   Istanbul   Karachi   Kolkata
Kuala Lumpur   Madrid   Melbourne   Mexico City   Mumbai   Nairobi
São Paulo   Shanghai   Taipei   Tokyo   Toronto

Published by Oxford University Press, Inc.
198 Madison Avenue, New York, New York 10016

www.oup.com

Oxford is a registered trademark of Oxford University Press

Library of Congress Cataloging-in-Publication Data
ISBN 0-19-510968-6 (text)
ISBN 0-19-516686-8 (instructor's manual)

1 3 5 7 9 8 6 4 2

Printed in the United States of America
on acid-free paper

Preface

This text presents a comprehensive overview of social welfare policy. It stresses the idea that because policy infuses every kind of social welfare practice, familiarity with social welfare policy is incumbent on every social worker. Blending this premise with an emphasis on the triggers of social change in social policy, the book develops a policy analysis model that highlights these themes. In its final section, it then applies this model to five core policy issues.

The instructor's manual mirrors the text's organization. It summarizes the basic content of each chapter and presents a variety of multiple choice, true/false, and discussion questions. The instructor can use these questions to lead classroom discussion as well as to prepare exams that test students' mastery of the material.

Learning social welfare policy requires that students know some facts and engage in ongoing dialogue with their instructor about social welfare policy concepts, values, and patterns. This manual is an instructional aid designed to promote that dialogue.

A special note of thanks goes to Diane Johnson, a doctoral student at the School of Social Welfare, Stony Brook University, who provided invaluable assistance in the manual's preparation.

Chapter 1

Introduction: Social Problems, Social Policy, Social Change

Summary: Students entering social work programs come with a variety of experiences and backgrounds, as well as a diversity of career goals. Yet, regardless of their initial interests, all soon find themselves asking the question, "Why won't the system let me do what I know is best for my client?" The first chapter addresses this issue by helping students to understand the structural impediments that undermine our ability to do our jobs and to understand the link between social policy and successful social work practice. After reading this introduction, students should have a clear understanding of how every form of social work practice embodies social policy and why social policy is such an essential subject for study.

Key Concepts: social policy, social advocacy, social problem, internal and external resources, evolutionism, cyclical theories, historical materialism, "grand" theories of social change, market economy, ideology, dominant ideology

Test Bank: The following questions have been designed to highlight the key concepts and ideas covered in this chapter. They may be used to test students' understanding of the material or to lead class discussions.

1. Social workers need to understand social policy because
      a. all social work agencies are involved in social advocacy.
      b. *an understanding of social policy helps us to use ourselves effectively as social workers.
      c. social work licensing exams are primarily based on social policy questions.
      d. none of the above.

2. The relationship between the definition of a social problem and social policy is
      a. social policies and social problems are both determined by Congress.
      b. *the definition of a social problem determines the type of social policies enacted to address the problem.
      c. there is no relationship between the definition of a social problem and social policy.
      d. a and b only.

3. Which of the following can negatively affect social work practice?
      a. poor program design.
      b. inadequate internal and external resources.
      c. conflicting objectives of social policies.
      d. *all of the above.

4. Social welfare policy can make it harder for social workers to do their jobs by
   a. limiting funding for certain social problems.
   b. restricting the ability of social workers to provide complete information about resources to clients.
   c. burdening social workers with such large amounts of paperwork that they are not able to serve as many clients nor access needed resources.
   d. * all of the above.

5. T*/F: Social policy is designed both to facilitate the goals of the social work profession and, at the same time, to impede their realization.

6. T*/F: To be an effective social worker, you must understand how social problems get constructed.

7. T/F*: In general, once social policies are formulated, they are rarely changed.

8. T*/F: Self-interest plays a part in the process whereby some issues get defined as social problems and others do not.

9. T*/F: There is a positive relationship between having political and/or economic power and the ability to define what is a social problem.

10. T*/F: Social policy affects the ease or difficulty with which we as social workers are able to do our jobs.

11. T*/F: An example of an external resource deficit is the lack of adequate housing for everyone who needs it.

12. T*/F: Knowledge of social policy can empower social workers in their day-to-day work with clients.

13. Discussion Question: How does the construction of a social problem help to create a social policy? Give some examples from your fieldwork internship.

    Answer: The way a social problem is defined foreshadows the definition of the olution. For example, if teenage pregnancy is defined as the result of the decline of the family and the spread of sexual promiscuity, then the solution will be defined as bolstering parental authority and encouraging teenagers to abstain from sex. From another perspective, however, if teenagers perceive that they have no real options for a future other than motherhood, then they will be unlikely to pursue education and will see no real reason to use birth control or abstain from sex.

14. Discussion Question: How do social policies shape what social workers do? Give some examples from your fieldwork experience.

Answer: As discussed in the previous question, social policies can directly influence the nature of the work that social workers do. Social policies can make it easier for social workers to do their jobs through respect for social workers' professional judgment and   provision of adequate resources and funding. Social policies can also make it harder for social workers to do their jobs by tightly controlling program guidelines, not providing adequate funds to meet program objectives, requiring a high volume of paperwork, and establishing conflicting objectives.

15. Discussion Question: How does a problem get to be defined as a "social problem" as opposed to an "individual problem"?

Answer: There are two ways:
   a. Those in power and/or those with a constituency (for example, the media) focus attention on a problem and identify it as a social need, that is, as a problem affecting many people, which needs a societal response in order to be solved.
   b. On a grassroots level, ordinary people may identify a problem they are experiencing and join with others who are experiencing the same problem to organize a social movement that brings the public's attention to the issue. This approach has been used to address issues of civil rights, workers' rights, unemployment insurance, etc.

16. Discussion Question: Discuss the relationship between self-interest and the definition of social problems.

Answer: How social problems get defined and the solutions put forth to correct these problems reflect the self-interest of the individual or group defining the problem. Therefore, not only is what gets defined as a social problem up for debate, but also how a particular problem is conceptualized. For example, is teen pregnancy caused by the decline of the family? By sexual promiscuity? By young women feeling trapped in low-paying, dead-end jobs? Or should it not even be defined as a social problem?

17. Discussion Question: In what ways might we argue that America's "war on drugs" is an example of the arbitary construction of a social problem? Give some examples to indicate how this definition of the problem represents the self-interest of certain groups.

Answer: We could argue that the "war on drugs" arbitrarily identifies some drugs as "bad," while it ignores the harmful effects of others. For example, crack and heroin are identified as "bad" drugs, are illegal, and those who are caught selling these drugs go to jail.   At the same time, alcohol and cigarettes are legal substances, even though both have been shown to have harmful effects on our health. Should not a "war on drugs," which has as its primary concern the health and well-being of its citizens, target all drug use? Should drug policy criminalize use or treat it as a health issue?

18. Discussion Question: Discuss how a social policy might make the job of a social worker more difficult.

Answer: Policies that restrict entitlements or eliminate services mean that there may not be adequate resources available to assist individuals and families with particular problems. For example, policies that emphasize punishment for drug offenders rather than rehabilitation may mean that there are not adequate rehabilitation programs available for all who need them.

19. Give an example of a current social policy that makes it more difficult for social workers to do their job.

Answer: Some examples are the Welfare Reform Act of 1996, establishing TANF, managed health care policies, assertive outpatient treatment policies in mental health, policies that require juvenile offenders to be treated as adults, etc.

20. Discussion Question: How have social workers employed in hospital settings been negatively affected by changing social policies during the past two decades?

Answer: Concerns about rising health care costs led to the imposition of diagnostic-related categories (DRGs) that established average length of hospital stays for various illnesses. Hospitals who failed to discharge patients "on time" received less reimbursement from insurance companies than those who discharged patients "on time" or early. The imposition of this policy changed the emphasis of a hospital social worker's job from finding the best setting to which to discharge patients as quickly as possible.

21. Discussion Question: What social policies in your field of social work practice have changed the nature of how social workers do their jobs?

Answer: Some fields of practice and policies include the following:
    a. mental health: assertive outpatient treatment policies.
    b. school social work: drop out prevention policies.
    c. mental retardation/developmental disabilities: aging out policies.
    d. geriatric care: eligibility policies.
    e. children and youth: family preservation policies.
    f. foster care: termination of parental rights policies.
    g. work with forensic clients: alternatives to incarceration policies.
    h. drug and alcohol clients: mandatory drug sentencing laws.
    i. domestic violence: mandatory arrest policies.

22. Discussion Question: Sometimes social programs seem to lack needed resources,

be poorly designed to meet an existing need, and have conflicting objectives. Blau suggests that these programs may be designed to fail. Why would government create programs that are designed to fail? What do you think about this issue?

Answer: Programs often get started because there is political pressure to respond to a social problem, but at the same time, there may also be conflicting political pressures to maintain the status quo.

23. The position of the National Association of Social Workers (NASW) with regard to social work practice includes all of the following EXCEPT
    a. a defining feature of social work practice is the profession's focus on individual well-being in a social context.
    b. social workers must work to promote social justice and social change with and on behalf of clients.
    c. advocacy is an essential part of social work practice.
    d. * individual clients' problems most often are intrapsychic and seldom involve attention to forces in the clients' environment.

24. T*/F: Most nineteenth- and twentieth- century theories of social change claimed that progress was an inevitable and inherent aspect of all human society.

25. All of the following are classic theories of social change EXCEPT
    a. historical materialism.
    b. * social learning theory.
    c. evolutionary theory.
    d. cyclical theories of change.

26. All of the following are aspects of evolutionism EXCEPT
    a. * a belief that history repeats itself.
    b. belief that the pattern of historical change propels society from primitive to more developed forms.
    c. a belief that stability and stagnation were the exceptions, not the rule.
    d. a belief that progress was the rule.

27. The theory of social change that claims history more closely resembles a circle rather than a straight line is
    a. historical materialism.
    b. chaos theory.
    c. evolutionism.
    d. * cyclical theories.

28. The theory of historical materialism is most closely associated with
    a. * Karl Marx.
    b. Otto Spengler.
    c. Auguste Comte.

    d.   Tony Blair.

29. The theory of historical materialism shares many common elements with which other theory?
    a. cyclical theories.
    b. trauma theory.
    c. * evolutionism.
    d. none of the above.

30. T*/F: At the core of historical materialism is a belief that through purposeful collective action workers can transform society.

31. T/F*: Sociologists today continue to believe in "grand" theories of social change.

32. T/F*: The author of this text, Blau, believes in the inevitability of human progress.

33. Blau argues that changes in social policy have their origins in which of the following arenas?

    a. the economy.
    b. politics and the structure of government.
    c. ideology and social movements.
    d. *all of the above.

34. T*/F: Having a model with which to analyze policy is important in order to be able to systematically analyze social policy.

35. T*/F: Blau argues that tensions within five arenas of society eventually give rise to conflicts that produce changes in social policy.

36. T/F*: The term "market economy" refers to a system for imitating the process of consuming.

37. T*/F: In the economic arena, social policy changes often result from the conflicting roles people find themselves in, each with a different set of needs.

38. Discussion Question: Blau argues that one of the most crucial functions of government in a market economy is the creation of an environment where business will prosper. What do you think about this argument?

39. Discussion Question: Blau argues that in addition to helping business prosper, government must promote a perception of fairness and that often these two tasks conflict. Do you agree with his argument? Why or why not?

40. Discussion Question: Blau argues that social welfare policy is often used to create programs that help government to combat the perception of unfairness in the social order and to maintain the status quo. Do you agree with his argument? Why or why not?

41. T/F*: Ideologies provide guidelines for defining how to overcome government policies.

42. Ideology is
       a. the worship of an idol.
       b. * a coherent set of beliefs about ideas, institutions, and social arrangements.
       c. the study of important ideas.
       d. the governing style of dictators.

43. T*/F: When a dominant ideology clashes with an alternative ideology, the resulting conflict and tension may result in changes in social policy.

44. The impetus for a social movement is usually
       a. an aspiration for life in a different geographic region
       b. a belief that society should control what people think
       c. social workers looking to promote their professional status
       d. * the identification of unmet needs of a group of people

45. T/F*: Social movements are usually free of tension and conflicts.

46. T*/F: When people look at historical precedents of successful social change, they are likely to feel empowered to fight for new social reforms.

47. T/F*: Overwhelming success characterizes the historical legacy of social welfare change in the United States.

Chapter 2

Definitions and Functions of Social Welfare Policy

Summary: To be effective social workers, students need to have an understanding of what social work policy is, how policy influences the agencies and programs for which they work, and how policy affects the day-to-day activities of the social worker in the field. This chapter begins with the traditional view of what policy is and, in particular, what social welfare policy is and argues that this traditional view is both too narrow and too simplistic. By the end of the chapter, students should understand how social welfare policy is embedded in economic, political, and social policies, as well as how any one policy performs social, political, and economic functions that often are at odds with one another. In addition, students should understand how social welfare policy has functioned to both assist and disempower particular groups of people in this country.

Key Concepts: social welfare policy, welfare state, safety net, fiscal welfare, corporate welfare, "non-decision" policy making, "deserving poor," "undeserving poor," pre-industrial society, industrial society, the social functions of social welfare policy, economic functions of social welfare policy, political functions of social welfare policy

Test Bank: The following questions have been designed to highlight the key concepts and ideas covered in this chapter. They may be used to test students' understanding of the material or to lead class discussions.

1. Social welfare policy can be defined as all of the following EXCEPT
    a. the way society responds or does not respond to social need.
    b. * institutional evidence of need.
    c. the principles, guidelines, and procedures that govern social agencies, universities, trade unions, and professional associations.
    d. policies that address both national and international issues.

2. Which of the following is an example of a social welfare policy?
    a. affirmative action.
    b. managed health care.
    c. immigration policy.
    d. * all of the above.

3. All of the following are TRUE about social welfare policy EXCEPT
    a. Social welfare policy can address economic, labor, and educational issues, as well as issues of poverty, entitlements, and health care.
    b. Social welfare policy and programs often benefit the affluent as well as the poor.
    c. * There is one definition of social welfare policy to which most social workers subscribe.
    d. Social welfare policy can be broad or narrow.

4. Discussion Question: What is meant by the term "welfare state"? Do you think the United States is a welfare state? Explain your answer.

> Answer: A "welfare state" is a society that makes the well-being of its citizens the responsibility of the government. An argument can be made that the United States is a welfare state because government addresses the well-being of the populace through programs such as free public education, the social security system, SSI, TANF, unemployment insurance, etc.
>
> Conversely, an argument can be made that the United States, during the twentieth and twenty-first centuries, is an example of a declining welfare state. For example, beginning with the Reagan presidency and continuing through the presidencies of George Bush, Bill Clinton, and George W. Bush, entitlement programs have been drastically cut back, modified, or eliminated, contracting the safety net that previously existed for citizens in need.

5. Which of the following is a TRUE statement?
    a. Social welfare policy refers to policies and practices affecting only private, not-for-profit agencies.
    b. Social welfare policy refers to the binding set of policies and procedures imposed by the federal government on all agencies providing services to the poor.
    c. * Social welfare policy is one type of public policy that deals with the principles, plans, and courses of action taken by the government on behalf of the larger society.
    d. none of the above.

6. Which of the following is a FALSE statement?
    a. In the United States, the government funds the private sector to deliver many social service programs.
    b. In Western European countries, the government operates most social service programs.
    c. The United States has a long history of funding private institutions to provide social welfare services.
    d. * President Franklin D. Roosevelt's social welfare reforms relied on private, not-for-profit agencies.

7. T*/F: In the 1980s and 1990s in the United States, all levels of government began to fund for-profit companies as well as not-for-profit agencies to provide social welfare services.

8. Discussion: Question: Do you think that social services should be able to be provided by for-profit companies and individuals as well as by not-for-profit agencies? Why or why not? What are some of the arguments used by social workers who oppose the provision of social services by for-profit entities?

Answer: In delineating the objections to for-profit agencies providing social services, the two main points are (1) that the profit motive will overshadow the needs of clients, and (2) that as government relies increasingly on the private sector to address social needs, it will see its role and responsibility for meeting these needs lessened.

9. Abramovitz criticizes the narrowness of the standard definition of social welfare for all of the following reasons EXCEPT
   a. The standard definition does not take "fiscal welfare" into account.
   b. The standard definition treats social welfare policy as a discrete entity when, in fact, it cannot be separated from other public policies that affect the well-being of individuals and families.
   c. * The standard definition represents the view of liberals and radicals.
   d. The standard definition does not take into account the fact that policy includes what the government does not do, as well as what it actually does.

10. Discussion Question: In the United States, some see the tax code as creating a system of "fiscal welfare" because our system of tax exemptions, deductions, and credits addresses the same needs as does direct government spending on social welfare needs. However, because the benefits of the tax code accrue mainly to the middle class and the wealthy, they conclude that, in reality, everyone is on welfare. Do you agree with this argument? Why or why not? What type of tax exemptions and credits benefit the middle and upper classes? Business owners? If everyone is truly receiving "welfare" of some type, why do you think poor individuals and families who must access programs like TANF and food stamps are so stigmatized?

   Answer: Review the types of tax exemptions, deductions, etc., that benefit the middle and
   upper classes as well as businesses and corporations. The issue of the stigmatization of recipients of TANF, food stamps, etc., is meant to challenge the notion that the poor are the only ones who receive government assistance and to provoke discussion about what makes some individuals and entities "deserving" of help and others "undeserving."

11. Critics cite all of the following as examples of "corporate welfare" EXCEPT
   a. employers' ability to deduct the costs of employees' health insurance and therefore lower their tax bill.
   b. government assistance in helping companies to advertise their products.
   c. government aid to assist companies in the construction of new facilities.
   d. *none of the above.

12. Discussion Question: Abramovitz highlights the argument of some that the government, by providing social welfare benefits, lessens the impact of inequality and therefore mutes social unrest and political disruption. Do you agree with this argument? Why or why not? Do you think that social workers, by virtue of our role advocating for and overseeing the administration and distribution of social welfare services, inadvertently play a role in

maintaining the status quo?

>   Answer: This question is intended to challenge students to think about the conflicting
>   functions of social workers and the ways we inadvertently may be working
>   against the very structural changes we believe are necessary.

13. We know that economic policy affects social welfare policy because
     a. economic policy directly affects funding for income maintenance programs such as
          TANF, social security, and unemployment insurance.
     b. during times of economic downturns, there are more people in need of cash assistance.
     c. when the government raises the minimum wage, the demand for cash assistance drops.
     d. * all of the above

14. Abramovitz makes all of the following points about the policy role of non-decision making
     EXCEPT
     a. Non-decision-making is a strategy employed by those in power to maintain the status
          quo.
     b. It is a means of defusing demands for change.
     c. * The people most hurt by non-decision-making are the leaders of the political party in
          power.
     d. Non-decision making often involves mobilizing bias against those calling for change.

15. The author criticizes the traditional definition of social welfare policy as
     a. too wordy and complex for most to understand.
     b. * too simple and too narrow.
     c. favoring the interests of big government and big business.
     d. none of the above.

16. All of the following are examples of harmful social welfare policies EXCEPT
     a. legalized slavery.
     b. * the 1964 Civil Rights Act.
     c. the 1871 Indian Appropriation Act.
     d. the 1882 Chinese Exclusion Act.

17. Which of the following groups has been hurt by harmful social welfare policies at some
     point in the history of the United States?
     a. Native Americans.
     b. African Americans.
     c. women.
     d. * all of the above.

18. Discussion Question: The author argues that it is vitally important to maintain an

awareness of the negative outcomes of certain social welfare policies, as well as an awareness of the instances when social welfare policies have been used deliberately to harm, disenfranchise, or disempower certain groups. Do you agree with her position? Why or why not?

> Answer: The arguments in favor of remaining aware of the negative effects of some social welfare policies center around two themes: (1) that outcomes of policies sometimes are very different from those anticipated and intended by the policy-makers, and (2) that there are numerous instances during the history of the United States when social welfare policies were used deliberately to disempower and disenfranchise certain groups. Awareness of these policy "failures" helps us to better anticipate obstacles to the successful implementation of policies and to speak out when policies are deliberately being used to oppress certain groups of people.

19. U.S. social policy in the nineteenth century created barriers to the full participation of women in society by
    a. barring women from voting.
    b. not allowing women to own property.
    c. not allowing women to receive credit in their own names.
    d. * all of the above.

20. Which of the following is a TRUE statement about laws and policies affecting lesbians and gay men?
    a. Sodomy laws forbidding physical expression of affection between persons of the same sex, even in their own home, still exist in one-third of states.
    b. The federal government openly discriminated against homosexuals in the civil service system until 1975.
    c. Social policy prevents most lesbians and gay men from being able to secure coverage for their partner on their health insurance policies.
    d. * All of the above.

21. T*/F: Ever since colonial times, women have been defined as deserving or undeserving of aid based on their marital status.

22. T/F*: U.S. social welfare policy has always deemed poor, single women and single mothers to be more in need of assistance than poor, married women and therefore has defined them as the "deserving" poor.

23. Discussion Question: Abramovitz argues that one theme running through social welfare policy throughout our history has been the hostility toward single mothers. What examples does she cite of policies that support her argument? What has been the experience of your clients who are single mothers when they have attempted to access benefits?

Answer: See the historical examples to support this view. The author argues that the most recent example of this hostility toward single mothers can be found in the harsh provisions of the 1996 federal welfare reform law known as Temporary Aid to Needy Families.

24. Which of the following is a TRUE statement?
    a. Social welfare policies in the United States have, at times, hurt as well as helped those in need
    b. Any one policy usually performs more than one function
    c. The social, political, and economic functions of a policy do not always share a common agenda
    d. * All of the above

25. Which of the following statements best indicates why some social policies hurt rather than help those they were intended to assist?
    a. Social policies are usually enacted by people who know nothing about the problem they are trying to solve.
    b. * The economic and political functions of a particular policy tend to favor the "haves," while the social functions benefit the "have-nots."
    c. Social policies are not usually well thought-out.
    d. None of the above.

26. Which best describes the social functions of social welfare policy?
    a. ensuring that individuals are good citizens
    b. promoting religious as well as the educational opportunities for families
    c. * enhancing the functioning and well-being of individuals and families
    d. preventing homelessness

27. Discussion Question: Over time, government has assumed greater responsibility for promoting individual development and preventing social problems. How does the author account for this shift?

    Answer: In general, it is important that students understand that the Industrial Revolution serves as the point of demarcation between a preindustrial society in which the family, the community, and the religious institutions carried out the tasks of socialization and an industrial society where these functions gradually began to be taken over by government because of the changing nature of the family, work, etc.

28. Discussion Question: In what ways does a conservative analysis of the social functions of social welfare policy differ from a liberal analysis?

Answer: In general, conservatives see the main role of social welfare's social functions as that of social control, i.e., regulating "deviant" and "irresponsible" behavior. This regulation of nonconforming behavior serves two functions: ensuring the smooth functioning of society and sending a message to the rest of society about the repercussions of nonconformity. In contrast, for liberals, the main role of social welfare is to promote individual development and family functioning and to cushion the effects of social problems.

29. Which statement best represents the radical and feminist analyses of the social functions of social welfare policy?
    a. Punishment works better than rehabilitation.
    b. Public policies should be used to alter or control the behavior of those who violate social norms.
    c. The social functions help to highlight the plight of the poor and the necessity of doing something about their situation.
    d. *The social functions of social welfare policy help to supply business and industry with obedient workers, families with compliant wives and mothers, and society with citizens who accept mainstream norms that favor the dominant class.

30. The economic functions of social welfare policy include
    a. guaranteeing a minimum level of economic security.
    b. supporting the maintenance of the family unit.
    c. stabilizing the economy during economic downturns.
    d. * all of the above.

31. Which of the following is a TRUE statement?
    a. Business and industry can provide employment for all those people willing and able to work
    b. The labor market serves everyone equally at all times
    c. Even during economic downturns, anyone who wants a job can find one.
    d. * Employment discrimination is one reason some people are not in the labor force.

32. Discussion Question: When discussing the economic functions of social welfare policy, policy analysts refer to its "automatic stabilizing" function. What do they mean? How does this work?

    Answer: See the discussion of the economic functions of social welfare policy. In general, during economic downturns, social welfare programs put cash into people's hands through cash assistance programs, thereby helping to "prime the pump" and keep business afloat. Because this money flows to business, it helps to stimulate the production of goods and services that, in turn, create jobs and reduce unemployment.

    32. T*/F: Radicals believe that social welfare policy operates to subsidize the costs of

profitable economic production for business and industry.

34. Radicals believe all of the following about social welfare policy EXCEPT
    a. * It enhances business profits by encouraging workers to purchase the products produced by their company.
    b. It enhances business profits by stimulating purchasing power.
    c. It enhances business profits by subsidizing wages.
    d. It enhances business profits by enforcing work norms.

35. Discussion Question: Radicals argue that one of the economic functions of social welfare policy is to promote business profits by ensuring the productivity of the workforce. What is the substance of their argument? Do you agree? Why or why not?

    Answer: Radicals argue that public spending on health, education, and social services ensures employers a healthy and fit workforce at virtually no cost to business. In addition, they argue that keeping social welfare benefit levels low and stigmatizing their use encourage people to choose any work, regardless of the wages paid or the working conditions, over receiving public assistance.

36. When feminists refer to the "social reproduction" function of social welfare policy, they are referring to
    a. the reproduction of the species.
    b. meeting the basic survival needs of individuals.
    c. rearing and preparing the next generation for adult work and family roles.
    d. * all of the above.

37. All of the following undermine the family's capacity for caretaking EXCEPT
    a. low earnings.
    b. * too many choices of consumer goods.
    c. substandard housing.
    d. inadequate health care.

38. Which of the following represents the conservative view of the economic functions of social welfare policy?
    a. Social welfare policy assists businesses by providing a "safety net" during economic Downturns.
    b. Social welfare policy increases the cost of doing business.
    c. Social welfare policy interferes with market functions.
    d. * b and c

39. T*/F: The political functions of social welfare policy address the need to reduce social conflict.

40. Social welfare policy helps to reduce interest group conflict by
    a. preaching the doctrine that all groups have equal access to resources.
    b. * distributing resources from those with more to those with less.
    c. encouraging those with less to work harder to get their "fair share" of existing resources.
    d. all of the above.

41. Radicals make which argument about the roots of interest group conflict?
    a. It comes from competition between interest groups over scarce resources.
    b. * It comes from the unequal structure of wealth and power that leaves many needs unmet.
    c. It has its roots in social Darwinism.
    d. Interest group conflict is promoted in families.

42. T*/F: Radicals argue that the provision of social welfare does all of the following EXCEPT
    a. reduces disruptive social protests.
    b. obscures the fact that governments often take the side of the "haves" over the "have-nots."
    c. hides the unequal and undemocratic nature of the social structure.
    d. * stimulates social conflict because citizens expect more than the system can provide.

43. The view that the welfare state helps both to legitimate the wider social order and to prevent demands for more extensive change is a position most likely to be taken by a
    a. * radical.
    b. conservative.
    c. moderate.
    d. reactionary.

44. Conservatives make all of the following arguments about social welfare policy EXCEPT
    a. It promotes a sense of "entitlement" on the part of the citizenry.
    b. *It legitimates the wider social order
    c. It fosters too much democratic participation.
    d. It raises to unrealistic levels citizens' expectations of what the government can do.

45. Discussion Question: Abramovitz argues that perhaps the best way to define social welfare policy is as an arena of struggle. What does she mean by this statement?

    Answer: The author argues that social welfare policy is not a static entity, but is the outcome of an ongoing process of debate, advocacy, and negotiation about the distribution of societal resources. This debate is ongoing because of different ideological views about the functions of social welfare policy and because of the often competing social, economic, and political functions of social welfare policies.

46. T*/F: Social welfare policies have the potential to strengthen the political and economic power of those with less.

47. Discussion Question: What argument does the author make to explain why the arena of social welfare policy is so hotly debated?

    Answer: The author argues that having access to income and services outside of work and marriage provides people with what they need to challenge the status quo, to fight to change how resources are distributed, and to organize to change the existing power structure of the society.

48. Discussion Question: The author notes that the history of the social work profession has reflected its location between the individual and society and has led social workers to feel that they must choose between adjusting people and programs to circumstances and to challenging the status quo. How do you respond to her observation? What has been your experience in your field internship of your social work role? Have you had to choose between these roles? Are these two roles mutually exclusive?

    Answer: This question is meant to help students "personalize" and to think about the often conflicting roles social workers are asked to play. Ideally, they will begin to wrestle with the question of how social workers can remain true to the ideals of social justice and helping to empower those with whom they work, while at the same time working within the constraints of agency dictates. Are these two goals mutually exclusive?

49. Social welfare programs in the United States fall into which two major categories?
    a. selective and competitive.
    b. * universal and selective.
    c. compartmental and income-based.
    d. deserving and old age.

50. Categorical social welfare programs
    a. * are designed to serve particular groups of people.
    b. are for everyone.
    c. are granted without demonstration of need.
    d. are very popular with conservatives.

51. All of the following are examples of universal social welfare programs EXCEPT
    a. * Medicaid.
    b. Social Security.
    c. Medicare.
    d. unemployment insurance.

52. Discussion Question: Abramovitz discusses social welfare programs that are universal and social welfare programs that are categorical. What are some examples of programs that are universal? What is the general public's perception of these programs? What are some examples of categorical programs? What is the general perception of these programs? Do you think the separation of social welfare programs into two different categories is a positive thing? Why or why not?

Answer: Many people hold one set of views about universal social welfare programs and another set of views about categorical programs. Most people regard universal programs (e.g., Social Security, Medicare, etc.) as important to their well-being and feel positive about the existence of these programs. On the other hand, many people hold negative impressions of the categorical programs (e.g., TANF, food stamps, Medicaid), regarding them as entitlements going solely to the poor that are funded out of the pockets of the rich and the middle class.

Chapter 3

The Economy and Social Welfare

Summary: Students often fail to understand the intersection of social and economic policy; they tend to see social welfare functions as something that stand apart from the marketplace. This chapter discusses the role of social welfare in the modern U.S. economy and discusses many economic terms that must be understood in order to have a good basis for understanding the relationship between economics and social welfare policy. In addition, we identify an important contradiction inherent in all social welfare policy: while social welfare policies are designed to protect people against the market, these policies also contribute to the market's profitability.

Key Concepts: economics, scarce resources, infrastructure, commodities, the market, monopoly, recession, depression, income inequality, wealth distribution, fiscal policy, monetary policy, entitlements, social spending, macroeconomics, microeconomics, factors of production, robber barons, monopoly, oligopoly, globalization, social structure of accumulation, supply and demand, equilibrium price, pure public goods, a sticky price, gross domestic product, rate of inflation, demand-pull inflation, cost-push inflation, productivity, poverty line, balance of payments, trade deficit, federal debt, business cycle, Gini ratio, antitrust suit, externalities, Federal Reserve Bank, regressive tax, progressive tax, social spending, discretionary spending, work ethic, downsizing, minimum wage, aggregate demand

Test Bank: The following questions have been designed to highlight the key concepts and ideas covered in this chapter. They may be used to test students' understanding of the material or to lead class discussions.

1. Discussion Question: This chapter highlights an important contradiction inherent in our political economy: social welfare stands in opposition to the marketplace, yet simultaneously enhances its functioning. What do the authors mean by this statement?

> Answer: The ways social welfare intersects with the economy both protect people against the deleterious effects of the market and, at the same time, contribute to the profitability of the market.

2. Discussion Question: Who were the "robber barons"? How did they transform the structure of modern business? Did they have a positive or negative impact? Explain.

> Answer: The robber barons were men who made vast fortunes in the early days of industrialization by creating monopolies in industries such as oil, steel, and railroads. As a result of the monopolies they created, by the early twentieth century, the two hundred largest nonfinancial enterprises controlled 49 percent of all corporate wealth. The corporations they created were not controlled by stockholders, but by management, effectively separating ownership from control.

3. Discussion Question: Many liberal and radical policy analysts have criticized the World Bank and the International Monetary Fund for the negative role they play in the world economy, but particularly in the economies of third world countries. What specific criticisms are leveled at the World Bank and IMF? What do you think about their role in the global economy? Explain.

> Answer: Criticisms of the World Bank and the IMF center on their demand that countries receiving aid restructure their economies around the needs of external financial interests. Often, countries receiving assistance must agree to allow foreign investment in their country, reduce social spending, privatize public utilities, and end land reform. In sum, the conditions of receiving assistance favor wealthy foreign corporations and hurt the indigenous population.

4. Discussion Question: Some policy analysts feel that the gross domestic product (GDP) is not a good measure of the overall functioning of the economy. What arguments do they make to support their position? Do you agree or disagree?

> Answer: Analysts critical of the usefulness of the GDP as a measure of the well-being of the economy point to the fact that the GDP includes the value of all goods and services delivered, even if some of those goods and services are the result of harmful manufacturing practices (for example, the cost of cancer treatments caused by industrial pollution). Thus, the GDP is not useful as a measure of the country's social health and well-being.

5. Discussion Question: What problems do policy analysts identify with the unemployment rate as it is presently calculated?

> Answer: The rate as currently computed does not take into account "discouraged workers," involuntary part-time workers, or those incarcerated in prisons.

6. Discussion Question: Why is the poverty line considered an "absolute" method of calculating poverty?

> Answer: The poverty line is considered an absolute measure because it measures poverty independently of what is happening with the rest of the population.

7. Discussion Question: Define the terms "balance of payments," "trade deficit" and "trade surplus" and indicate what they tell us about the economy. Do you think these are useful measures of our economic well-being? Why or why not?

> Answer: Balance of payments, trade deficit, and trade surplus are all terms that identify the amount of money flowing out of a country for imports versus the amount of money coming into a country through exports.

8. Discussion Question: Describe the cycle that economists refer to as the business cycle.

> Answer: Economists label the natural patterns of a market economy the *business cycle*. At its height, the market prospers for a while until profits shrink and growth begins to slow. Then workers' wages stagnate, some lose their jobs, and the economy begins to deteriorate until it hits bottom. Eventually, however, the cycle turns upward as businesses gradually begin to identify investment opportunities, hire more workers, and produce more goods.

9. Discussion Question: How does the author account for the tremendous wealth and income inequality in the United States? Do these factors support or refute the argument that "a rising tide raises all boats"?

> Answer: One factor cited is that of the huge jump in compensation for corporate CEOs. During the boom of the 1990s, CEOs earned an average of 531 times more than the pay of the average worker. This example refutes the conservative argument that "a rising tide raises all boats."

10. Discussion Question: Some policy analysts have criticized the Federal Reserve Bank as being antilabor and pro-business. What arguments do they make to support this position? Do you think this is a valid argument?

> Answer: Critics of the Fed point to the fact that when unemployment is low and wages are rising, the Fed will most often raise interest rates as a way to puncture the upward pressure on wages. The Fed justifies these actions on the basis of curbing inflation, but some analysts feel it is much more an example of a pro-business/antilabor position.

11. Discussion Question: What are some of the factors that contributed to the development of the market economy during the past hundred years?

> Answer: These factors include inventions such as the internal combustion engine; the availability of capital for investment; the development of the assembly line, which revolutionized production; the use of advertising to create a market for consumer products; and the control of labor and unions by corporations and the government.

12. Discussion Question: What is the efficiency versus equality argument that some economists make when talking about the relationship between social welfare and the economy? What is the counterargument made by other economists? Give some examples.

> Answer: The argument they make is that to promote greater equality in the market means to sacrifice some of the market's efficiency. The counterargument is that promoting equality in the market not only does not diminish the market in any way, but actually

makes it work better. For example, ending discrimination of all types eliminates the waste that occurs when talented and gifted individuals are unable to secure jobs or are underemployed because of discrimination.

13. Discussion Question: The author argues that the public sector is essential to the growth of the private sector and that the two grow together. How does the author support his argument?

Answer: This argument centers on the large social costs that result from the growth of the private sector and that must be borne by the public sector. For example, "costs" such as pollution, unemployment and the need for an expanding infrastructure to support a developing private sector all fall on the public sector.

14. Discussion Question: Blau cites five factors that help us understand why the boom economy of the 1990s benefited some and not others. Identify and discuss these five factors.

Answer: The five factors the author identifies are downsizing, the role of trade unions, the decline in value of the minimum wage, the increase in low-wage work, and the growth of part-time and temporary labor. See the text for an elaboration of each of these factors.

15. Which of the following have to do with economics?
    a. the use of scarce resources.
    b. the production of valuable commodities.
    c. the distribution of goods among different people.
    d.* all of the above.

16. All of the following are ways social welfare intersects with the economy EXCEPT
    a.* by seeking to control supply and demand for goods.
    b. by reducing economic insecurity.
    c. by promulgating regulations that protect the health and safety of the citizenry.
    d. spending by government on the public infrastructure.

17. Which of the following is an example of social policy trying to be more "market-like"?
    a. building in a cost-of-living increase for welfare recipients.
    b. increasing recipients' food stamp allotment during good economic times and reducing their allotment during times of economic downturn.
    c. * instituting mandatory work requirements for welfare recipients.
    d. all of the above.

18. When we use the term "market economy," we mean
    a. an economic system by which the government sets prices.
    b. * an economy in which most commodities produced are for sale on the open market with the hope of making a profit.

c. an economy in which the amount of profit businesses can earn is capped.

d. none of the above.

19. A market economy characterized by extensive markets and a universal right to private property is unique to
- a. socialism.
- b. feudalism.
- c. * capitalism.
- d. communism.

20. The term "factors of production" means
- a. the amount of money needed to produce a particular commodity.
- b. the amount of profit made on the sale of a particular commodity.
- c. * the process whereby land, capital and labor are combined to produce goods.
- d. the process whereby the preferences of consumers are taken into account in the production of goods.

21. The most powerful exception to the notion of "voluntary exchange" in a market economy is
- a. the stock market.
- b. the bond market.
- c. the real estate market.
- d. * the labor market.

22. Until the late nineteenth century, most businesses were
- a. corporations.
- b. * small, family-owned enterprises.
- c. subsidized by the government.
- d. highly profitable.

23. An example of a monopoly is
- a. an industry that sells more goods than other industries.
- b. a company that is owned by one family and has no shareholders.
- c. * a corporation that effectively dominates or controls an industry.
- d. none of the above.

24. An oligopoly is
- a. a corporation that controls a particular industry.
- b. * an industry that is controlled by several companies.
- c. a company owned by several generations of one family.
- d. none of the above.

25. Globalization refers to all of the following EXCEPT
    a. * the ability of individuals to travel in ever shorter periods of time from one country to another.
    b. the increasingly global nature of the world economy.
    c. the dominant role of the United States in the world economy.
    d. huge shifts in financial capital and currency trading.

26. One of the negative consequences of globalization is
    a. the rapidness with which information can be transferred
    b. the shorter amount of time allowed for the production of goods
    c. * the depression of wages caused by competition from different countries
    d. none of the above

27. The principle of "less eligibility" is
    a. a system of evaluating those applying for welfare against one another to determine who receives assistance and who does not.
    b. is another term for the "unworthy poor."
    c. a term used to describe the criteria for receiving public assistance in most states in the South.
    d. * a requirement that someone receiving public assistance must have a lower standard of living than the worst-paid worker.

28. An "equilibrium price" is
    a. the point at which supply is greater than demand.
    b. the point at which demand is greater than supply.
    c. * the point at which supply and demand balance out.
    d. none of the above.

29. Which of the following affects demand for a particular commodity?
    a. the price of the item.
    b. the price of related goods.
    c. individual tastes and preferences.
    d. * all of the above.

30. In general, we can say that
    a. * if supply is greater than demand, the price falls.
    b. if supply is greater than demand, the price rises.
    c. if demand is greater than supply, the price falls.
    d. none of the above.

31. Economists define a "sticky" price as
    a. one that is very elastic and responds to market changes quickly.
    b. * one that fails to respond quickly to changes in demand.

    c. a price consumers feel is a "fair" price and therefore they refuse to pay more.

    d. none of the above.

32. The two exceptions recognized by economists to the forces of supply and demand are

    a. goods produced in sweatshops and entitlement programs.

    b. goods exported to foreign countries and "sticky" prices.

    c. goods purchased from foreign countries and the public infrastructure.

    d. * "sticky" prices and pure public goods.

33. When economists talk about "pure public goods," they mean something that is characterized by all of the following EXCEPT

    a. one individual's use of a public good does not interfere with its enjoyment by another.

    b. the benefits of a public good cannot be targeted at particular people.

    c. * a public good is beneficial to citizens in many countries simultaneously.

    d. no individual acting alone can decide how much of a public good should be purchased.

34. All of the following are examples of a public good EXCEPT

    a. the weather service.

    b. a lighthouse.

    c. * the services of a not-for -profit agency serving children and adolescents.

    d. a system of national defense.

35. The gross domestic product (GDP) is

    a. * the sum of all the paid goods and services produced in the U.S. economy.

    b. an indicator of our country's social health.

    c. the sum of all products produced for households.

    d. an indicator of the balance between our imports and exports.

36. All of the following are types of unemployment recognized by economists EXCEPT

    a. frictional.

    b. structural.

    c. cyclical.

    d. *proportional.

37. An economic period in which the GDP shrinks in two consecutive quarters and unemployment is between 6 percent and 10 percent is defined as

    a. a period of stagflation.

    b. * a recession.

    c. a depression.

    d. a period of inflation.

38. When economists refer to "externalities," they mean
    a. factors outside of the factory that affect whether the products get on the market quickly.
    b. *a cost or benefit that is not reflected in the immediate cost of the transaction.
    c. the marketplace where a particular item will be sold.
    d. none of the above.

39. Which of the following is NOT an example of an externality?
    a. pollution.
    b. * raw materials.
    c. public health.
    d. literacy.

40. When is government most likely to try to stimulate aggregate demand?
    a. * when the economy is down, and unemployment is rising.
    b. when the economy is booming, and there is a shortage of labor.
    c. when the economy is in a period of inflation..
    d. when by strong labor unions predominate.

41. The Federal Reserve Bank is most concerned about
    a. recession.
    b. depression.
    c. unemployment.
    d. * inflation.

42. The Federal Reserve Bank is one of our most important economic institutions because
    a. it has more money than any other bank.
    b. * it sets the interest rate that determines the cost of money throughout the economy.
    c. its chairperson is a very powerful person.
    d. one of its primary responsibilities is formulating the federal budget.

43. The Federal Reserve Bank can control the supply of money by doing all of the following EXCEPT
    a. setting the discount rate.
    b. changing the amount of money banks have to keep on hand at any one time.
    c. * controlling the amount of new money minted by the Treasury Department.
    d. buying and selling government bonds.

44. A regressive tax is
    a. one that taxes the rich at a higher rate than it taxes the poor.
    b. a tax imposed on property.
    c. * a tax that taxes the rich and poor at similar rates.
    d. a tax that carries over on the books from a previous administration.

45. All of the following are examples of regressive taxes EXCEPT
    a. * property tax.
    b. tax on cigarettes.
    c. tax on liquor.
    d. tax on clothing.

46. Fiscal policy is
    a. what the government spends and the interest rate on the money government has to borrow.
    b. * what government takes in through taxes and what it spends on social programs, education, the military, etc.
    c. how much money is in circulation and who has what amount of money.
    d. how much money is in circulation and how much of it is invested in the stock market.

47. All of the following are examples of mandatory spending EXCEPT
    a. * money spent to maintain our national parks.
    b. money spent to fund Social Security.
    c. money spent to fund Medicare.
    d. money spent to fund Medicaid.

48. Until the late nineteenth century most needs of the family such as food, shelter, and education were provided by
    a. the government.
    b. * the family.
    c. neighbors.
    d. the church.

49. All of the following are TRUE statements EXCEPT
    a. * The transition to a market economy took wealth out of the hands of the "robber barons" and put it in the hands of the middle class.
    b. The transition to a market economy transformed the social structures of society.
    c. The transition to a market economy drastically altered the way people lived.
    d. The transition to a market economy eventually gave rise to the modern welfare state.

50. Critics of relying solely on the market to meet all basic human needs make the argument that
    a. the government can do a better job than the market in meeting these needs.
    b. the family can do a better job than the market in meeting these needs.
    c. some people are lazy and therefore won't be able to get what they need.
    d. * market economies have always paid some people less than they need to survive.

51. All of the following are examples of ways the public sector subsidizes the private

sector EXCEPT
   a. tax incentives for job training.
   b. publicly funded research.
   c. * corporate loans for those going to business school.
   d. the establishment of an industrial zone to promote economic development.

52. Which best characterized the economy of the 1990s in the United States?
   a. a manufacturing based economy.
   b. a stagnant economy.
   c. * a service economy.
   d. a depressed economy.

53. All of the following are TRUE about the minimum wage EXCEPT
   a. It establishes a floor for other wages.
   b. 62 percent of those receiving a minimum wage today are women.
   c. Since 1968, the minimum wage has not kept pace with inflation.
   d. * The minimum wage guarantees that everyone will be able to purchase the basic
       necessities of food, shelter, and clothing.

54. During the past twenty-five years, the dominant economic model in the United States has
     been characterized by all of the following EXCEPT
   a. * tighter regulation of business and industry.
   b. low unemployment.
   c. less social welfare.
   d. less government intervention.

55. T*/F: From the early 1970s through the terrorist attack of September 11, 2001, U.S.
     policymakers tried to make social policy more market-like.

56. T/F*: The term "microeconomics" is used to discuss the economy as a whole.

57. T*/F: In a precapitalist society, land, capital, and labor were not for sale.

58. T*/F: An underlying belief of all transactions that occur in a market economy is that each
     transaction occurred at a "fair" price.

59. T*/F: Market economies are based on the premise of a "voluntary exchange."

60. T/F*: In a market economy, it is true that the market for labor is roughly equal to the market
     for goods.

61. T/F*: The percentage of the economy that comes from government spending is roughly
     equivalent in the United States and in Western European countries.

62. T/F*: Large corporations have pretty much bought out or wiped out small businesses in the United States

63. T/F*: Small business in the United States. today is both politically and economically influential.

64. T/F*: Globalization affects the manufacturing sector of the economy in same way it affects the service sector.

65. T*/F: Perceptions of political stability influence business investment.

66. T*/F: The term "social structure of accumulation" means that different systems of production and different socioeconomic institutions characterize different kinds of economies.

67. T*/F: The United States in the twenty-first century can best be characterized as a postindustrial service-based economy.

68. T*/F: Microeconomics is most concerned with how prices are set.

69. T/F*: The gross domestic product (GDP) is a straightforward and unambiguous measure of how the economy is functioning.

70. T/F*: The unemployment rate is a measure of how many people are receiving unemployment insurance.

71. T*/F: Demand-pull inflation occurs when the total demand for goods rises more rapidly than the economy's productive potential.

72. T*/F: Cost-push inflation occurs when costs rise despite high unemployment and a reduced use of resources.

73. T/F*: The federal debt is synonymous with the budget deficit.

74. T/F*: In the United States, inequality of income and inequality of wealth have been reduced in recent years.

75. T*/F: According to data for the year 2000, compared to other modern economies, the United.States is the nation with the greatest income inequality.

76. T/F*: The purpose of an antitrust suit is to try to end the use of vouchers for religious and parochial schools.

77. T*/F: The Federal Reserve Bank oversees monetary policy in the United States.

78. T*/F: When economists talk about government "priming the pump," they mean that government is spending money it doesn't have.

79. T*/F: The primary sources of government revenues are taxes.

80. T*/F: The federal income tax is an example of a progressive tax.

81. T/F*: By the year 2001, a significant share of the tax burden was shifted from local and state governments to the federal government.

82. T*/F: The growth and dominance of the market economy is one of the most remarkable changes of the past one hundred years.

83. T*/F: One of the most important effects of the Industrial Revolution and the growth of the market economy for the development of contemporary social welfare was the increasing number of people who labored, and got paid a wage, working for someone else.

84. T/F*: Most workers in the United States in the year 2000 worked for themselves in small businesses.

85. T*/F: Social welfare spending is sometimes referred to as an attempt to redirect wealth from the "haves" to the "have-nots."

86. T/F*: Data indicates that everyone benefited equally from the economy of the 1990s.

87. T/F*: Downsizing is a phenomenon that affects only blue-collar workers.

88. T/F*: During the past half century, the number of workers in trade unions has steadily increased.

89. T/F*: Conservatives are usually in favor of increases in the minimum wage.

90. T*/F: In the United States in 1999, 33 percent of all women with jobs earned poverty-level wages.

Chapter 4

The Politics of Social Welfare Policy

Summary: Like economics, the politics of social welfare policy goes a long way toward defining a policy's essential features. But what exactly is "politics" and how does it help us to answer the question, "Who should get what?" Drawing on ideas from political science, this chapter discusses the basic features of our political system. An emphasis on its conceptual underpinnings helps students understand the relationship between the functioning of this political system and the creation of social welfare policy. In addition and just as important, this chapter addresses the issue of social change. Students learn that to be effective advocates for social change, they must grasp the interplay of politics and policy. Skillful use of this knowledge is vital if they are to succeed in fighting to implement social policies that affirm the worth of every human being.

Key Concepts: politics, electoral activities, nonelectoral activities, interest group pluralism, public choice theory, elite theory, Marxist elite theory, direct democracy, indirect democracy, representative democracy, federalism, judicial review, bureaucracy, a system of checks and balances, "soft" money, "hard" money, divided government, critical elections, Morone's theory of the cycle of social reform, "American exceptionalism"

Test Bank: The following questions have been designed to highlight the key concepts and ideas covered in this chapter. They may be used to test students' understanding of the material or to lead class discussions.

1. Interest group pluralism is a model of power based on all of the following EXCEPT
    a. interest groups are a part of American politics.
    b. all interest groups have roughly equivalent power.
    c. * only the fittest survive.
    d. the U.S. government is a neutral institution, balancing interests on a case-by-case basis.

2. The conservative response to the decline of pluralism was
    a. * public choice theory.
    b. radical theory.
    c. systems theory.
    d. survival of the fittest theory.

3. Public choice theory makes all of the following arguments EXCEPT
    a. individuals benefit through "mutual exchange."
    b. a reliance on markets helps to avoid a surplus of goods.
    c. individuals always seek to maximize their gains.
    d. * what benefits those at the top will "trickle down" to those below.

4. A key premise of public choice theory is
    a. the concept of the individual does not really exist.
    b. everyone in a democracy makes decisions based on the collective good.

    c. the economic premise of scarce resources is a myth.

    d. * all policy decision making should make at least one person better off without making anyone worse off.

5. A theory that criticized pluralism from the left was
    a. neofascism.
    b. *elite theory.
    c. chaos theory.
    d. libertarian theory.

6. All of the following reflect the political views of most American political scientists EXCEPT
    a. There is no ruling class in the United.States
    b. U.S. society is an open society where anyone can rise to the top.
    c. * Society is organized to benefit primarily the interests of one class.
    d. Conflict in society occurs between groups, not between classes.

7. To be truly democratic, representative democracy must meet all of the following standards EXCEPT
    a. popular sovereignty.
    b. *political equity.
    c. political equality.
    d. political liberty.

8. What type of government system do we have in the United States?
    a. an oligarchical system of government.
    b. a decontextualized form of government.
    c. a totalitarian form of government.
    d. * a federal system of government.

9. Federalism derives its authority from
    a. * the Constitution.
    b. the Declaration of Independence.
    c. the Gettysburg Address.
    d. George Washington's Farewell Address.

10. Critics of federalism make all of the following points EXCEPT
    a. There are no national standards for things like education, pollution and welfare.
    b. Investors can leave a jurisdiction and go to another if they do not like the laws in one area.
    c. It is hard to bring about social change in a federal system of government.
    d. * There are no checks and balances under a federal system of government to prevent one branch of government from becoming too powerful.

11. Under the U.S. system of government, who has responsibility for advising the president and directing the affairs of the federal agencies under his or her control?
    a. the vice president
    b. the speaker of the House of Representatives.
    c. * the cabinet members.
    d. the Senate majority leader.

12. The way the U.S. Senate is structured gives disproportionate power to
    a. the more populous states.
    b. * the states with less population.
    c. the richer states.
    d. the poorer states.

13. The principle of judicial review
    a. requires that the president have on his staff several lawyers to review all legislation that the president sends to Congress for a vote.
    b. * grants the courts the power to decide if a law is constitutional.
    c. allows the courts to veto presidential orders.
    d. suggests that the legislative branch consult with the judicial branch.

14. The historic Supreme Court decision in 1954 that ordered schools to be desegregated was
    a. *Marbury v. Madison*
    b. *McCulloch v. Maryland*
    c. * *Brown v. The Board of Education*
    d. *Roe v. Wade*

15. Which of the following is true about how judges make their decisions?
    a. They do not like to make decisions that will put them in the position of administering a social agency or monitoring an agency's compliance with a court order.
    b. Before making a decision, they consider the extent to which new decisions alter judicial precedents and overturn prior legislation.
    c. They try to determine what specific policy consequences follow from a judicial decision and how these decisions will affect future administrative discretion.
    d. * All of the above.

16. The two largest departments in the U.S. federal bureaucracy are
    a. * Defense and Veterans' Affairs.
    b. Health and Human Services and Defense.
    c. Housing and Urban Development and Education.
    d. Labor and Health and Human Services.

17. In the United States, one of the greatest problems of government bureaucracy is
    a. corruption in the civil service system.
    b. * an underlying belief that government should never be allowed to "outdo" the private sector.
    c. incompetence of the workforce.
    d. all of the above.

18. Social workers need to be concerned about the structure of the federal bureaucracy because
    a. the general public perceives social workers as bureaucrats.
    b. many private, not-for-profit social work agencies depend on the federal bureaucracy for their funding.
    c. the trend is for all social work programs to be funded by the Department of Health and Human Services.
    d. * the federal bureaucracy is often responsible for overseeing the administration of federal social welfare programs in the states.

19. All of the following are features that make the U.S. system of government different from that of other countries EXCEPT
    a. the role of political parties in the U.S. system.
    b. the low rate of voter participation in the United States
    c. * the amount of corruption in the U.S. government.
    d. the U.S. system of divided government.

20. The U.S. political system can be described as
    a. * a winner-take-all model.
    b. a proportional representational system.
    c. a collective system.
    d. all of the above.

21. All of the following are characteristics of "critical elections" EXCEPT
    a. realignment of the majority and minority grouping within the parties produces a new majority.
    b. *a candidate who was considered a "dark horse" wins his or her party's nomination.
    c. the realignment with the majority and minority parties lasts for a long time.
    d. a new ruling coalition is created from the political majority.

22. Social workers need to pay attention to Morone's theory of the cycle of social reform because
    a. he has proven that the cycle happens every fifty years.
    b. he is regarded as one of the greatest social theorists.
    c. his theory helps us to understand why Democrats are the most effective social reformers.
    d. * his theory can help to prevent the erosion of hard fought social gains and a return of the old political equilibrium.

23. All of the following are distinctive aspects of the U.S. political structure EXCEPT
    a. *a widely recognized class structure.
    b. the absence of a significant socialist or labor party.
    c. a belief in individualism and equal opportunity.
    d. a weak trade union movement.

24. T*/F: The author defines "politics" as all the political actors, institutions, and activities involved in the process of governing.

25. T*/F: Interest group pluralism is based on a belief that power is noncumulative.

26. T*/F: Public choice theory applies market principles to nonmarket decision making.

27. T*/F: A capitalist state ultimately depends on a profitable capitalist economy.

28. T*/F: Marxist elite theory is often criticized for the false dichotomy it sets up: that either capitalism is replaced or every kind of intermediate social reform simply bolsters its position.

29. T*/F: A direct democracy is in which there is no intermediate level of government between the ruler and the ruled.

30. T*/F: Indirect democracy requires the election of a group of people who determine state policy.

31. T/F*: In the United States today, we have primarily a direct form of democratic government.

32. T*/F: Under a federal system of government, national, state, and local authorities all share power.

33. T/F*: Over the past two hundred years, the dominant trend in the United States has been toward a curbing of presidential powers.

34. T*/F: The U.S. Congress consists of the Senate and the House of Representatives.

35. T/F*: The population of the state determines the number of seats a state has in the U.S. Senate.

36. T/F*: The House of Representatives is identified as the legislative body that is supposed to slow the pace of social change.

37. T*/F: The branch of U.S. government given the power to declare war by the Constitution is

the legislative branch.

38. T*/F: The judiciary is a coequal branch of the federal government.

39. T*/F: The principle on which the U.S. Supreme Court relies for its decisions is *stare decisis,* that is, let the court's preceding decision on the issue stand, unless there is a compelling reason to reverse it.

40. T*/F: In the United States, both judge-made law and legislative law are viewed as equal.

41. T*/F: In general, we can say that judges and the justice system move cautiously.

42. T*/F: One of the difficulties inherent in bureaucracies is measuring performance.

43. T*/F: The two- party system in the Unites States is quite unusual compared to what exists in other countries.

44. T/F*: Over the past twenty-five years, the differences between the political parties in the United States have grown.

45. T*/F: "Soft" money is the money that individuals and corporations donate to national and local political parties, rather than to individual candidates.

46. T*/F: The concept of "American exceptionalism" refers to the aspects of the U.S. political structure that set it apart from many other countries.

47. Discussion Question: There are both supporters and critics of the pluralist theory of political decision making. What are the main arguments of those who favor a pluralist approach? What are the main arguments of those who criticize pluralism? Where do you stand on this issue?

    Answer: Those who favor a pluralist model of political decision making argue that (1) the interest group system is democratic because groups are easily formed and the government is willing to listen to the views of any group, and (2) interest groups are the best way for "the people" to convey to politicians what they want on a day-to-day basis.

    Those who criticize pluralism argue that (1) the interest group system is not democratic because not all groups wield equal power; (2) the interest group system is biased toward the interests of the upper class and the private sector; and (3) pluralism de-emphasizes issues such as distributive justice, equality, eradication of poverty, and unemployment.

48. Discussion Question: Give some examples of both electoral and nonelectoral activities that are part of what the author defines as "politics."

Answer: Electoral activities include everything from voting on election day to amending state constitutions, passing referenda, and "recalling" or removing an elected official before the completion of a term. Nonelectoral activities include lobbying, petitions, demonstrations, strikes, and boycotts, all of which are designed to show support for or against a particular administrative action, policy, pending legislation, or enacted law. The author's intent is to have students broaden their view of what is meant by the term "politics."

49. Discussion Question: There are a number of criticisms that can be made of public choice theory. What are they?

Answer: Public choice theory can be criticized for all of the following:
a .its argument that the state does not exist.
b. its argument that people act only to maximize economic gain.
c. its argument that individuals act to maximize personal gains. Yet, public choice theory
   y applies this argument only to issues of health, education, and public assistance. It does not relate this theory to defense or other policy areas that conservatives favor.

50. Discussion Question: What is the main difference between pluralism and elite theory?

Answer: Pluralism argues that the ruling minority always changes, that is, one group is victorious on one issue, and another group is victorious on the next issue. Elite theory, on the other hand, argues that although different interest groups may win on particular issues, the status quo never changes because a real transfer of power never takes place. Regardless of what happens on any single issue, those in power retain that power.

51. Discussion Question: What arguments does Marxist elite theory make?

Answer: This type of elite theory assumes the existence of a ruling class that derives its power from its position in a capitalist economy. Its proponents argue that because the state in a capitalist society must remain responsive to the economically dominant class, the ruling class does not have to exercise direct power. As long as a capitalist state must depend on a profitable capitalist economy, the state will side with business interests on most issues.

52. Discussion Question: Blau identifies a long-standing debate among political scientists about the nature of democracy. What are the two sides in this debate?

Answer: One side in this debate holds that a government is democratic if its procedures are democratic. These procedures include universal participation, political equality, majority rule, and responsiveness to public opinion. According to this argument, it is not the outcome that matters, but whether the procedures allow most people to participate in decision making.

The other side in this debate argues that not only must the procedures be democratic, but democracy must also be apparent in what government actually does, for example, in freedom of religion and in meeting human needs.

53. Discussion Question: What are the four domains in which the president, under the U.S. democratic system, takes responsibility?

Answer: These four domains of the president are often referred to as the four "subpresidencies." They include:
a. foreign policy.
b. economic policy.
c. other domestic policy functions.
d. symbolic/moral leadership.

54. Discussion Question: Blau describes the history of the Supreme Court as being characterized by two competing tensions. What are these tensions? Give some examples of each.
Answer: The two competing tensions identified by Blau are
a. the Court in an activist role where its decisions extended certain rights and required certain actions. Examples of the Court's activist role are seen in *Brown v. The Board of Education, Goldberg v. Kelly*, and *Roe v. Wade*.
b. the Court in an obstructionist role where its decisions were intended to prevent other institutions from doing something, such as intruding too much on property rights or otherwise intervening in the economy.

55. Discussion Question: Blau notes that the way the judicial system functions and how justices make their decisions is part of the larger debate among scholars and jurists about the proper way to interpret the Constitution. What are the three basic positions in this debate? Which position do you agree with? Why?

Answer: The three basic positions in the debate over how to interpret the Constitution are

a. The "original intent" theory asks, what did the drafters of the Constitution intend when they wrote it? Did they see the judicial branch in an activist role? An obstructionist role? The preservation of the status quo? This theory is the least interventionist.

b. The "living Constitution" theory sees the Constitution as a document that demands new interpretations in order to change with the times. This theory is the most interventionist.

c. The "plain meaning of the text" theory contends that judges should seek to determine what the Constitution says. This theory is the "middle of the road" position that allows the courts to justify a moderate degree of activism.

56. Discussion Question: What is a bureaucracy? What are its distinctive features? What types of tasks does a bureaucracy handle well? What types of situations are usually not handled well by bureaucracies?

Answer: A bureaucracy is a large organization in which people with specialized knowledge are divided into a clearly defined hierarchy of bureaus, each with a specialized mission.
   The distinctive features of bureaucracies include
a. a chain of command.
b. a formal set of rules to guide behavior.
c. advancement based on merit.

Bureaucracies are supposed to be able to carry out complex tasks and function best when the tasks are big and repetitive. Bureaucracies often do not function well when the problem or issue they face deviates sharply from what they have been programmed to manage.

57. Discussion Question: What experiences have you had with bureaucracies? What kinds of experiences have your clients had with bureaucracies? When you have had a problem with a bureaucracy, how have you handled the problem? When your clients have had trouble with a bureaucracy, how have they handled the problem? What might account for some differences between how you handled a bureaucratic problem and how your clients have handled bureaucratic problems?

Answer: This question is designed to get students thinking about issues of power and perceived powerlessness, differential access to resources, issues of race, class, etc., and how these issues affect each individual's sense of empowerment and potential efficacy in promoting change.

58. Discussion Question: Blau notes that the present-day functioning of our political parties has deep roots in the American system. Explain.

Answer: Blau cites the work of social policy analysts Piven and Cloward, who remind us that the Founding Fathers were largely members of the landed aristocracy who feared that political parties opposed to the interests of the propertied class could mobilize the populace. To blunt this possibility, the Founding Fathers created a system of "checks and balances" that effectively divided authority among Congress, the presidency, and the judicial system. This system restricted the influence of political parties over government by fragmenting the authority of the central government and, in effect, creating serious obstacles to political party organization and power.

59. Discussion Question: Blau cites a number of possible reasons that voter participation is

so low in the United States. What are these reasons? Why do you think the percentage of people who vote is as low as it is? Do your clients vote? Why or why not?

Answer: Blau cites a number of reasons why Americans may have disengaged from the political process:

a. Some may feel that the choices they are offered are false ideological choices--for example, being forced to choose between a candidate who supports equality for women or a candidate who supports the traditional family, when what most want is *both* of these things.

b. A feeling that government is run by "a few big interests."

c. A feeling of apathy and contentment with the way things are.

d. Neither the Democrats nor the Republicans have put effort into mobilizing more voters because they have not seen it as in their best interest to do so. Mobilizing poor people represented too great a risk because they would make demands in exchange for their vote.

60. Discussion Question: What are the arguments for and against a divided government?

Answer: Those in favor of divided government argue that this structure, where power is shared among many, prevents the abuse of power and makes it difficult to get an absolute majority. By impeding the formation of an absolute majority, this structure slows down the pace of social change, just as the Founding Fathers intended.
     Those opposed to a divided government point to the "political paralysis" that results from the separation of powers and the system of checks and balances, along with a decentralized and fragmented bureaucracy. They argue that the Founding Fathers' obsession with preventing the abuse of absolute power is overshadowed in the twenty-first century by the disabling consequences of the protections they built into the system.

61. Discussion Question: Blau identifies just four elections in U.S. history that can be characterized as "critical elections." What were these elections?

Answer: The four "critical elections" were the following:
a. The first occurred in 1860 when the North elected Lincoln,the first successful Republican candidate, and brought about the Civil War.

b. The second occurred in 1896 when Republican business interests in the East defeated populist attacks on monopolies and the railroads, leading to a business/monopoly dominance that lasted for more than three decades.

c. The third occurred in 1932 with the election of Franklin D. Roosevelt. FDR's election brought poor and working people into the Democratic Party and cemented a New Deal coalition that lasted until 1968.

d. The fourth occurred in 1968 with the election of Richard Nixon, who ran against the civil rights reforms of the Great Society and brought blue-collar workers into the Republican Party.

62. Discussion Question: Political scientist James Morone has developed a theory about the cycle of social reform to complement the theory of critical elections. His theory posits the existence of a "democratic wish." What is Morone's theory and what does he mean by the "democratic wish"?

Answer: Morone's theory posits that Americans hold a mythic belief that they do not really need a government to govern themselves. According to this view, all government should resemble a small New England town meeting. Because Americans hold this view, Americans have never adequately equipped the federal government with the needed authority to do its job.

Morone's theory describes four stages that constitute the cycle of social reform:

a. Political stalemate characterizes the first stage. This stage is broken when the pressure for change mounts to a certain level and the proponents of change invoke the "democratic wish": the belief that our problems could be solved if only we would listen to "the people."

b. The second stage occurs when Americans respond to the call to listen to "the people," attack the status quo, and demand empowerment.

c. The third stage occurs when the profile of previously oppressed groups is raised and new institutions are established to address the problems of these groups. Yet these institutions do not have the power to translate the mythic call of "the people" into real accountability and effective governance.

d. Therefore, in the fourth stage, the old political equilibrium is soon reestablished.

63. Discussion Question: Blau addresses the political functions that social welfare performs. What are these?

Answer: Social welfare has the capacity to perform dual functions: it can heighten the demands for social change and help to secure these changes, and it can also function to mute the demands for social change.

64. Discussion Question: Blau argues that to be successful social workers, we need to

understand the larger political environment in which social workers function. What points does Blau make?

Answer: A central element of social work is the commitment to expand choice and opportunities for all. Because of the structure of the U.S. political system, this is not an easy task. Blau argues that if we are to succeed, we need to pay attention to four criteria for any new program:

a. a program must increase the capacity of the government to address human needs, that is, it must make the bureaucracy less fragmented and more efficient.

b. for legislation to be enacted, a program must link this increased capacity with broad congressional support.

c. the benefits the program delivers must go to a diverse group of citizens.

d. the program must provide these benefits without a means test.

Chapter 5

Ideological Perspectives and Conflicts

Summary: As a system of beliefs that explains the structure of society, ideologies and ideological conflicts have existed for a very long time. Yet the nature of ideology and the way it can affect our daily lives are rarely discussed. For social workers, in particular, it is very important to have an understanding of how ideology affects both social welfare policy and social work practices. The answers to questions such as who should receive social work services, how eligibility is determined, what services should be universal, etc., all reflect the ideological values of those formulating the policies. By the end of the chapter, students will come to understand the issues of power and how the structure of inequality influences explanations of reality. The chapter therefore explores different perspectives representing the interests of specific groups in society about human need, the role of government, the characterization of human nature, the meaning of work, and the nature of the family, as well as explanations of racial inequality.

Key Concepts: ideology, dominant ideology, human nature, social conservatism, laissez-faire conservatism, neoclassical liberalism, pragmatic liberalism, humanistic liberalism, radicalism, liberal feminism, cultural feminism, socialist feminism

Test Bank: The following questions have been designed to highlight the key concepts and ideas covered in this chapter. They may be used to test students' understanding of the material or to lead class discussions.

1. Ideology can be defined as
     a. the prejudices and biases people hold about others.
     b. beliefs that are based on ideas.
     c. * a relatively coherent system of beliefs held by individuals and groups about human nature, institutional arrangements, and social processes.
     d. the study of ideas.

2. Which of the following statement is true of ideology?
     a. Ideology is fluid and complex.
     b. Ideology is embedded in individual belief systems and wider social values.
     c. There are many different ideologies.
     d. * All of the above.

3. Individuals and groups may reject the beliefs and values of the dominant ideology for all of the following reasons EXCEPT
     a. Their life experiences have led them to reject the dominant view and to subscribe to other social values more consistent with their own experiences.
     b. The mainstream ideology denies them access to power.
     c. *The dominant institutions socialize them to challenge the dominant ideology.
     d. The mainstream ideology denies them economic rewards.

4. All of the following are TRUE statements about ideology EXCEPT
    a. * The dominant ideology expresses the beliefs and values of the people, rather than of those in power.
    b. Everyone is influenced to some degree by the dominant ideology.
    c. The ideological messages received from the wider society become so pervasive that we tend to take them as "truth."
    d. The dominant ideology shapes our thinking and behaviors until these beliefs are challenged by another way of thinking.

5. All of the following are arguments in favor of unionization of social workers EXCEPT
    a. Social workers need to recognize that they have an economic relationship to their place of employment.
    b. Collective bargaining agreements can help social workers win salaries commensurate with their professional status.
    c. Unionization connects social workers with the broader political arena.
    d. *Unionization guarantees social workers higher status and professional prestige.

6. The stakes are high in ideological debates about social welfare policy for all of the following reasons EXCEPT
    a. * Social welfare policy decisions are seen as a harbinger of an upcoming election
    b. Social welfare policy decisions affect many people's lives.
    c. Social welfare policy decisions influence the distribution of scarce resources.
    d. Social welfare policy will determine who pays for and who benefits from government action.

7. All of the following are arguments used by opponents of unionization of social workers EXCEPT
    a. *Unions tend to be antimanagement.
    b. Unionization conflicts with the notion of professionalism and public service.
    c. Unionism is unnecessary in nonprofit agencies.
    d. Unionizing conflicts with the image of the selfless social worker.

8. Feminist criticisms of social work include all of the following EXCEPT
    a. The profession's knowledge base needs to be broadened to include the social construction of gender, the impact of gender inequality, and the effect of the wider social context on problems faced by women.
    b. Women's leadership roles in the profession needs to be more highly valued and emphasized.
    c. *There are not enough women in the profession.
    d. The question of power needs to be addressed by social work as an institution.

9. T/F*: Republicans are always conservative and Democrats are always liberal.

10. T*/F: Most individuals' thinking contains elements of more than one ideological

perspective.

11. T/F*: Ideologies always remain constant.

12. T*/F: At any given point in time, there is one ideology or set of beliefs that supports the status quo and whose supporters regard as "truth."

13. T*/F: Ideology is useful for providing an interpretation of the world as it is and for developing an idea of how the world should be.

14. T/F*: It is always easy to identify the ideological messages underlying our thoughts and beliefs.

15. T/F*: The prevailing ideology furthers the interests of everyone in the society.

16. T*/F: Ideological messages conveyed through institutions are not "neutral" messages.

17. T*/F: It is not uncommon for those in power to try to co-opt ideological challenges by incorporating some of these alternative beliefs into the mainstream ideology.

18. Discussion Question: Abramovitz refers to having an ideology as like having a road map. What does she mean?

Answer: Abramovitz likens ideology to having a road map because just as a road map indicates our whereabouts, so too does ideology provide us with a framework for understanding the surrounding world. Our values and beliefs about the "how" and "why" of everyday events help us to make sense of the relationship between the individual and society They also aid us in formulating an agenda for social action.

19. Discussion Question: Where do we get different ideological messages? Give some examples of the types of ideological messages we get.

Answer: All of us get ideological messages from our families, from schools, from religions, from other institutions, from our peers, from mass media, popular culture, etc. These ideological messages help to define societal gender roles, the structure of families, the importance of work, the nature of religious beliefs, "proper" behaviors, etc. For example, in American society, boys and girls learn that one of the things they are expected to do when they become adults is marry someone of the opposite sex. In addition, most young girls grow up with a belief that they should have children. Students will be able to identify many other "messages" they got growing up that reflect the prevailing ideology.

20. Discussion Question: Abramovitz notes that mainstream ideology defends and rationalizes a society's particular social, legal, moral, religious, political and economic arrangements. She cites several ways this happens. What are these ways and what are the implications of these processes for social workers?

Answer: There are four ways the dominant ideology defends and rationalizes the status quo:

a. spelling out social norms and stigmatizing any behavior that deviates from these norms.
b. blaming social problems on individuals without taking into account the larger social conditions.
c justifying social inequities rather than identifying these inequities as problems to be addressed by the larger society.
d. suggesting in many ways that the existing status quo is "natural," "inevitable," beneficial, and as it should be.

The implications for social workers are many. In general, when social workers understand the ways in which the dominant ideology reinforces the status quo, including the inequities built into the system and reinforced by societal institutions, they can begin to help clients develop a critical consciousness and become empowered to challenge the individual and social obstacles to equality and fulfillment of their potential.

21. Discussion Question: What are different ways in which individuals and groups may resist mainstream ideas or "take on the system"?

Answer: There are many ways that individuals and groups can and do demonstrate their opposition to the ideas and values of the dominant ideology: through participation in social movements; organized protests; supporting political candidates who hold different views; running for office on a platform of opposition to the beliefs of those in power; supporting alternative newspapers and magazines; rejecting the mainstream use of language; manner of dress, etc.; and adopting a nontraditional or alternative lifestyle.

22. Discussion Question: Abramovitz identifies several key questions in social welfare policy where ideological differences can result in very different approaches to the provision of social welfare. What are these key questions?
Answer: (see text) The questions identified by the author are:
a. What is the character of human nature?
b. What is the relationship of the individual to society?
c. How should need be determined?
d. What role should government play in the provision of social welfare?
e. What is the meaning of work?
f. What is the nature of the family?
g. How should racial inequality be interpreted?
h. What are the benefits of professionalism?

You may wish to have the students make a large chart with these questions down one side and conservative, liberal, radical and feminist ideologies running along the top. Have the students fill in the answer to each question for each ideology. Note: the author does not address the question of the benefits of professionalism using this framework. In addition, some of the topics are discussed using different variations of these overall perspectives. You can adapt the chart according to your lecture.

	conservative	liberal	radical	feminist
human nature?				
relation of individual to society				
what is need?				
role of government?				
meaning of work?				
what is family?				
why racial inequality?				

(1) Views of Human Nature:

a. Social Conservatism: grounded in religion; believes humans are creatures of God who are marked by original sin, driven by uncontrollable passions and unable to be trusted to be masters of their own fate. Society must restrain individuals by bringing them under the moral authority of God, family, church, and government.

b. Laissez-Faire Conservatism: has unlimited faith in the ability of humans to control their own destiny. Believes individuals are rational, competitive, self-interested and able to self-regulate. Without undue restraint from external forces, individuals will maximize success.

c. Pragmatic Liberalism: holds the same view as laissez-faire conservatism except does not believe that an unfettered market will necessarily maximize human success. Therefore, wants society to recognize the impact of social conditions on the capacity of individuals to compete for success.

d. Humanistic Liberalism: individuals are rational and autonomous, but also altruistic, dependent, and interdependent. Relationships with others help individuals become autonomous, but autonomy doesn't eliminate an individual's dependence or need to help others. Human beings are social beings who live and work in cooperation with one another.

e. Radicalism: human nature is socially constructed through the interplay of human biology, the physical environment, and human society. Human labor is central to their view of human nature (as opposed to the capacity to reason), because radicals see human nature as the product of human activity. Humans consciously and intentionally engage in physical labor directed to transforming the material world so it will satisfy basic needs. Human nature varies with specific historic conditions: it reflects the mode of production (capitalism, feudalism, socialism, or communism) and the individual's location in society's class structure.

f. Liberal Feminism: disputes the belief that women are not rational human beings and therefore inferior to men. Argues that any observed differences in human nature between men and women are a reflection of sex role socialization, not some innate difference between the sexes.

g. Cultural Feminism: holds two views of human nature: (1) that male-female differences and the subordination of women are rooted in nature, particularly in the biological division of labor, and (2) that patriarchy, the system based on male domination and female subordination, socially constructs human nature. Therefore, they argue that the existing categories of "woman" and "man" are neither "natural" nor "eternal," but are ideologically constructed to define women as inferior and men as superior.

h. Socialist Feminism: argues that the system of capitalism, patriarchy, and racism play a role in shaping human nature. Also believes that there is a relationship between human labor and human nature and that the gendered division of labor supports a system of male domination and female subordination.

(2) Relationship of the Individual to Society:
    a. Social Conservatism: believes that the well-being of individuals and society depends on restricting the freedom of individuals and controlling their behavior. Security, support, and nurture require using the law, social norms, and distribution of resources to enforce duty, proper behavior, and social obligation. They believe that the general welfare depends on individual compliance with the moral authority of God, the patriarchal authority of the family, and the mandates of the state.

b. Laissez-Faire Conservatism: believes that the well-being of individuals and society depends on ensuring individual autonomy and independence and maximizing their ability to compete for success. Individuals must be left alone with a minimum of control or interference from others.

c. Pragmatic Liberalism: believes that large differences in income and wealth mean that everyone does not have the same chance for success. Therefore, they believe that government needs to "level the playing field," making equal opportunity a possibility for everyone.

d. Humanistic Liberalism: believes that individuals do best in relationship to others. Therefore, they believe that the policies of society must reflect the importance of the interdependence of people and must promote cooperation, mutuality,and the collective welfare, as well as the welfare of the individual.

e. Radicalism: emphasizes the alienation of people from one another, from their work, and from their environment, which stems from a capitalist economy. The resulting societal divisions based on race, class, and gender must be eliminated and replaced by an egalitarian, classless society committed to meeting the needs of all citizens.

f. Liberal Feminism: stresses that promoting the general welfare means that gender inequality must be eliminated. Women must have equal opportunity to participate fully in all societal institutions. Therefore, sexist practices that deny women equal opportunity must be eliminated.

g. Cultural Feminism: like liberal feminism, cultural feminism stresses that promoting the general welfare means that gender inequality must be eliminated. However, cultural feminism emphasizes that male domination in all spheres of life must be eliminated to end the oppression of women.

h. Socialist Feminism: argues that the intersection of gender, race, and class governs the individual's relationship to society. Therefore, promoting the general welfare requires changing the current gendered division of labor in the workplace and in the home, altering the ideology that supports this gendered division of labor, and eliminating all forms of domination based on class, gender, and race.

(3) Definition of Need:
   a. Social Conservatism: believes that people know what they need and have all of the information required to make an informed choice. Therefore, people buy what they need and need what they buy. Thus, consumer demand constitutes "need." They do not acknowledge any gap between needs and resources and therefore oppose nearly all

forms of government intervention in the economy.

b. Laissez-Faire Conservatism: same as social conservatism.

c. Pragmatic Liberalism: like laissez-faire conservatism, believes that an individual's interaction with the market defines need. Yet pragmatic liberalism also believes that there are those who do not have the financial means to buy what they need. It therefore rejects the belief that market behavior alone accurately reflects need. Supports government setting a standard of need below which no one should be expected to live. Equates liberty with freedom from want—essentially, a guaranteed minimum standard of living and calls on government to make sure that all reach this level. It does not, however, advocate great changes in the prevailing distribution of income and wealth.

d. Humanistic Liberalism: takes a broader definition of need: need is made up of what one needs to guarantee physical survival plus access to social rights. Social rights are the rights of citizenship that one accrues by virtue of membership in the community, for example, the right to make decisions, compete for success, have access to information to make informed choices, the right to develop relationships, to have leisure time, and to pursue personal interests. Without access to these social rights, individuals will not be able to live a full life according to prevailing societal standards.

e. Radicalism: argues for a social or collective definition of need not determined by market dynamics. One's basic needs are defined as those things one needs to participate fully in society. Therefore, a central social value is the distribution of societal resources according to need.

f. Liberal Feminism: broadens the meaning of need to include personal and societal needs for care. Argues that care is a universal aspect of human life, that we need care to thrive and develop our full capacities.

g. Cultural Feminism: same as liberal feminism.

h. Socialist Feminism: same as liberal feminism.

(4) Role of the Government:

a. Social Conservatism: sees important role for government in controlling "deviant" societal forces such as crime, homosexuality, and abortion, while deploring active role of government in fostering the secularization of American institutions.

b. Laissez-Faire Conservatism: strongly opposes government intervention in the economy and most other social arenas, especially the regulation of business; acknowledges necessary albeit minimal role for government in assisting only the most needy by assisting them to get back to work.

c. Pragmatic Liberalism: endorses limited government intervention to assist individuals and families. Believes government should consistently mediate the market's rough edges by correcting the negative impact of the market economy on individual and family well-being.

d. Humanistic Liberalism: sees a broad role for the government in ensuring civil, political, and social rights as a means to maximize all citizens' participation and integration into the society. The government should take necessary steps to decrease inequality that exists as a result of market fluctuations and processes.

e. Radicalism: sees the role of government as acting entirely in the interests of the owners of production (capitalists) and the dominant class. Therefore, remains skeptical about positive role of government in alleviating poverty. Characterizes the needs of capitalism and the state as in direct opposition to those of workers and the people in general.

f. Liberal Feminism: sees government as a neutral arbiter of conflicting social interests and as an ally in efforts to increase the equality between men and women. Highlights the existence of male bias in existing institutions, including those charged with assisting women affected by market forces. Sees important role for government in ensuring all women's access to equal opportunity, pay equity and child care, etc.

g. Cultural Feminism: sees the government as more or less an arm of the patriarchy. Fosters an approach to welfare that encourages independence when at all possible from government. Advocates self-help and collective organizations.

h. Socialist Feminism: has the most developed critique of the role of government. Believes that the government represents the interests of capitalists and the patriarchy and therefore reproduces and reinforces unequal power relations based on gender, race, and class.

(5) Meaning of Work:

a. Conservatism: glorifies the work ethic. Sees work as consistent with God's plan and characterizes nonwork as deviant, lazy, and immoral. Considers efforts to assist nonworkers with financial assistance as promoting dependence and contrary to underlying social Darwinist assumptions of "survival of the fittest."

b. Liberalism: argues that people work because it serves a range of social, psychological, and economic needs. Explores human elements related to work as important as the needs of the job in shaping the workday, work context, and content.

c. Radicalism: believes that work allows individuals to develop their human potential and interconnectedness. Values work not only for its results but also for the process involved. In a capitalist society, however, work is the primary context of exploitation and domination of the workforce.

d. Liberal Feminism: focuses on unequal treatment of women in the workplace and unequal distribution of household tasks among women and men. Calls attention to the need to eliminate barriers to ensure equal opportunity and equal pay.

e. Cultural Feminism: sees the hierarchical structure of the workplace as controlled by men in order to dominate women. Calls for eliminating male-dominated hierarchies in the labor market and at home.

f. Socialist Feminism: sees the gendered division of labor as designed to benefit capitalism and patriarchy by disadvantaging women. Economic insecurity resulting from low wages and lack of power allow for the subordination of women in the home and on the job.

g. Feminists of Color: distinguish the struggle for equality of women of color from the struggle of white feminists. Because of the history of slavery and racial inequality, women of color have had no separation of work and family.

(6) Nature of the Family:

a. Social Conservatism: regards two-parent, heterosexual family as natural and unchanging social unit and as the bedrock of society. Believes that men, not women, should run the family and that traditional religious morality should cement the family's social bonds. Believes that big government has weakened the family by usurping its traditional authority and by supporting single-parent households. Calls on the government to exert moral leadership to restore traditional family values.

b. Laissez-Faire Conservatism: agrees with social conservatism, except that it wants to preserve the family to promote individualism, rather than for moral reasons.

c. Pragmatic Liberalism: challenges the idealized notion of the family and does not see the "traditional" nuclear family as natural and inevitable. Sees the family as a social, rather than a biological group. Therefore, acknowledges the value of diverse families and fosters family policy that supports different family structures. Advocates for government supports for families such as affordable child care, flexible work hours, etc.

d. Humanistic Liberalism: same as pragmatic liberalism, except adds to the family policy agenda family allowances, higher public assistance grants, afterschool programs, programs for battered women, etc.

e. Liberal Feminism: calls for women to have the same rights to autonomy and self-determination in the home as society grants to men, thereby requiring a restructuring of gender roles for both men and women. Advocates for men to increase their role in child rearing and housework and for women to expand their roles from wife and mother as their potential allows. Calls for quality child care, equal pay, and family medical leave.

f. Cultural Feminism: regards the family as patriarchal and predicated on heterosexuality, male authority, compulsory motherhood, and the domination of women by men, especially women's identities, bodies, and sexuality. Calls attention to patterns of inequality and conflict in the family, often resulting in high rates of divorce, incest, rape, marital rape, and battering. Cultural feminists therefore put issues of abortion, rape, and male violence against women on the public policy agenda.

g. Socialist Feminism: emphasizes men's control over women's domestic labor and the ways this benefits both capital and patriarchy. Women's domestic services free employers from having to purchase the same services on the open market. Sees motherhood in capitalism as essential to the socialization of future workers. Some call for household work to be paid through public benefits.

h. Feminists of Color: stress the role of racial stratification in shaping family life. Highlight the effects of oppression in denying people of color the same family structures that have functioned as buffers for whites in the society. See adaptations of the family structure resulting from racism as evidence of strengths rather than failure.

(7) Interpretation of Racial Inequality:

a. Social Conservatism: relies on theories of natural and fundamental differences to explain racial inequality. Asserts that inequalities result from cultural inferiority and reflect moral and cultural deficits. Strongly opposes Affirmative Action.

b. Laissez-Faire Conservatism: explains inequality as resulting from lack of human capital, irrational behavior of business, or rational discrimination based on the statistical odds.

c. Pragmatic Liberalism: sees racial inequality as resulting from prejudice and racial discrimination. Calls for equal treatment under the law and policies to eliminate barriers responsible for discrimination.

d. Humanitarian Liberalism: holds that despite legislative, judicial, and constitutional progress, a deeply entrenched racial divide systematically advantages whites at the expense of persons of color. Declaring that equal opportunity is an insufficient remedy, it supports policies such as affirmative action to redress inequality.

d. Radicalism: argues that racial inequality reflects both the social construction of the meaning of race and the existence of institutionalized racism. Sees fundamental equality resulting from legal efforts to address institutional racism and the redistribution of power to end white supremacy.

23. Discussion Question: There are five distinguishing features of the standard model of a profession. What are these features? Describe potential problems associated with each feature.

Answer: The five features are
a. knowledge based on a systematic body of theory acquired through training.
b. authority derived from specific professional expertise.
c. a professional culture consisting of values, norms, and symbols.
d. community approval to perform special services over which the profession has a monopoly.
e. a regulative code of ethics.

The following are the potential problems associated with these features:

a. Social work knowledge base: criticized for leaning too heavily toward individual explanations of social behavior, mainstream interpretations of social institutions, and an uncritical acceptance of social work's social control functions. Sends a message that individual clients, not the wider social structure, are responsible for personal distress.

b. Authority derived from a specific professional expertise: because people typically associate expertise with power, can turn into a rationale for controlling clients. Clients may be encouraged to conform to values and goals to which they do not subscribe. Clients who disagree with the professional may be labeled as "resistant" "lacking insight," etc. Class, race, gender, and sexual orientation differences between worker and client can further exacerbate these differences. Emphasis on technical competence favors working on a narrow set of issues and discourages dealing with the whole person.

c. Professional Culture:
    Behavioral Norms: There are three major behavioral norms that characterize the provision of social work services: Each of these has potential problems:
        1. impersonality: may minimize the client's role in decision making and reduce self-determination.
        2. objectivity: encourages social workers to remain neutral about the social forces that contribute to individual and social problems and to separate professional work and social reform.
        3. impartiality: social workers sometimes criticized for failing to honor impartiality to the fullest.
    Ethic of Service: Service ideal promotes ethic of selflessness mandating that social workers put the needs and interests of clients before their own or

their agency's interests. Problems arise when clients
1. perceive social workers valuing monetary rewards over providing good services.
2. perceive social workers using client's confidences for personal gain.
3. perceive social workers value professional prestige and personal reward over clients' interests.

d. Community Approval: Need for community sanction, combined with the need for paying clients, outside funding, and government support may induce professionals to abide by goals and values of those with the most power. Licensing requirements may exclude valuable expertise of paraprofessionals and community residents. Licensing, by definition, establishes social workers as an exclusive group that may distance them from both their clients and other workers.

Chapter 6

Social Movements and Social Change

Summary: Usually, when individuals try to solve a problem or seek relief from a hardship, they act on their own. Yet collective action—the efforts of individuals joining to promote social change—is nonetheless central to the development of modern societies. A key tenet of the social work profession is the belief that people acting together have the power to affect and reshape the social order. This chapter highlights the role of collective behavior as a force for social change and introduces students to both the classical and the newer theories of social movements.

Key Concepts: collective action, individual resistance, social protest, social movements, "the personal is political," crowd theory, psychoanalytic social movement theory, mass society theory, structural strain theory, the theory of the underclass, structural functionalism, paradigmatic shift, rational crowd theory, relative deprivation theory, status strain theory, political opportunity structures theory, rational choice theory, free rider concept, resource mobilization theory, new social movement theory, Marxist theory, socialist feminism, racial formation, racialization, collective action frames, master frames, free social spaces

Test Bank: The following questions have been designed to highlight the key concepts and ideas covered in this chapter. They may be used to test students' understanding of the material or to lead class discussions.

1. T*/F: The social work profession believes that by acting in concert, people have the ability to affect and reshape the public realm.

2. Discussion Question: What role did collective action play in the expansion of the welfare state in the United States?

    Answer: Over a period of many years, social reformers from many walks of life joined forces with members of oppressed groups to fight for public awareness and redress of issues of poverty and discrimination. Their efforts included (1) defining issues as social problems, (2) developing a vision of possible resolutions to the problems, and (3) fighting for social justice.

3. A common element of all collective action is
    a. going on strike.
    b. boycotting a particular company's product.
    c. * groups of people pooling their resources to achieve common ends.
    d. engaging in violent uprisings.

4. Discussion Question: What are some of the changes that can result from engaging in collective action or participating in a social movement?

Answer: In general, when people join together to fight for a common goal, their challenges to the system (1) change attitudes, (2) broaden citizenship, (3) expand democracy, and (4) help to secure needed structural changes.

5. Discussion Question: Throughout history, collective action has played a significant role in many social changes and social policy advances. Identify and describe some of these important social changes and social policy advances that have been influenced by collective action throughout America's history.

Answer: Many social policy advances and important social changes have occurred during the course of American history as a result of collective action. For example, from 1896 to 1914, the Progressive Era coalition pressed the government for reforms regulating big business, shortening the work day and supporting mothers' pensions. During the 1930s, President Franklin D. Roosevelt responded to the many protests at relief offices and the activism of trade unionists and political radicals in responding to the Great Depression. The passage of the Social Security Act was, at least in part, in response to these organized demands for change. More recently, the civil rights movement has influenced the passage of many antidiscrimination laws. In addition, the women's movement, the gay rights movements, and the disabilities movement also have advanced the civil rights of previously disenfranchised populations.

6. T/F*: Collective actions are always liberal in nature.

7. T*/F: By individual acts of resistance, Abramovitz is referring to the small, personal, daily strategies resorted to by most marginalized members of society in an effort to counter the forces of oppression.

8. Discussion Question: What do feminists mean by the phrase "the personal is political"? Does this concept have applicability to the clients with whom you work?

Answer: Feminists use the phrase "the personal is political" to mean that every aspect of daily life embodies the mechanisms of oppression that are a part of the larger sociopolitical-economic system. By linking the personal with the political, feminists have helped to create a "politics of lifestyle" in which people seek the right to be different and the right to sustain community.

9. T/F*: Social protest and social movements are the same thing.

10. Which of the following is characteristic of social protest?
    a. resistive action on the part of an individual.
    b. *usually spontaneous, short-lived and involves the use of unconventional tactics.
    c. depends on a long-lasting, formal organizational structure.

d. all of the above.

11. Discussion Question: What argument do Piven and Cloward make about the importance of social protest?

    Answer: Piven and Cloward's study of protest movements in the 1930s and 1960s concludes that social protest is an especially important political resource for those who lack access to other sources of political power, such as individual influence, organizational standing, foundation support, and access to political leaders.

12. Discussion Question: Piven and Cloward argue that the structure of power in society, which favors those at the top of the class pyramid, restricts the type of political action available to low-income people. Abramovitz, drawing on the work of Piven and Cloward, states, "Even when poor and working-class communities play by the rules, they cannot gain much political influence, given the political system's bias toward the haves over the have-nots. Therefore, poor people's movements—those with few resources and limited access to centers of power–must resort to the politics of disruption that defy political norms to achieve their ends." Do you agree? Why or why not?

13. A factor that helps to prevent the poor and working classes, in particular, from engaging in social protest is
    a. mounting frustration over the conditions of their lives.
    b. fear of political reprisal.
    c. lack of interest.
    d. * a belief, reinforced by the system, that we all deserve our lot in life.

14. T*/F: The historical record shows that protest politics have been a main resort of those who lack other institutional forms of political access and influence.

15. T*/F: The historical record shows that during major crises, political leaders confronted with mass protest have met at least some of the protestor's demands.

16. Piven and Cloward suggest that the politics of defiance and disruption work better than conventional strategies for the poor because of all of the following EXCEPT
    a. *The poor don't know how to use conventional strategies of social change.
    b. It is easier for those in power to ignore demands for change when protestors use conventional methods.
    c. Disruptive activities challenge the dominant group's vision of a satisfied public.
    d. Protests galvanize public attention, force bystanders to take a stand on contested issues, and create divisions that pose a threat to the established powers.

17. In looking at successful social protests, Piven and Cloward note that social protest leaders often are faced with

a. pressure to tone down their activities.

b. pressure to form traditional movement organizations.

c. pressure to reintegrate themselves into regular political channels.

d. *All of the above.

18. All of the following are characteristics of social movements EXCEPT

a. the presence of formal organizations with an identified membership.

b. *a spontaneously evolved series of protest actions.

c. a degree of longevity.

d. represents a challenge to existing arrangements of power.

19. T/F*: The social movement as a form of mass mobilization and means for social transformation has existed as long as human history.

20. Abramovitz argues that concessions granted to social protestors and social movements over time

a. have hurt attempts to expand the welfare state.

b. * have contributed significantly to the rise and expansion of the welfare state.

c. have had nothing to do with the welfare state.

d. have alienated a large segment of the population.

21. Discussion Question: Abramovitz points to three contradictions that have sparked much activism in the United States. during the twentieth century. What are these contradictions?

Answer: The following are three contradictions the author cites:

a. the promise of equal opportunity in a democratic society and the denial of that equal opportunity because of ongoing discrimination based on race, gender, class, and other characteristics.

b. an economy based on production for profit for a few, while many others are forced to live with basic needs unmet.

c. the controlling and liberatory possibilities of the welfare state.

22. T*/F: People become politically active when conditions violate widely held class or cultural norms about what the market should provide.

23. The crowd, psychoanalytic, mass society, and structural strain theories share all of the following characteristics EXCEPT

a. *They represent the current state of the art regarding collective action.

b. They all focus on the behaviors and motivations of individuals who are seen as impulsive and deviant.

c. They regard all forms of collective behavior as spontaneous, contentious, and socially pathological.

d. They fear this form of behavior could threaten a sound, stable, and established way of life.

24. Discussion Question: What are the main tenets of Gustave Le Bon's crowd theory?

Answer: Le Bon argued that civilization rests on the ability of a small intellectual elite to impose discipline and rationality on the rest of the people. Democracy is seen as threatening this task because it unleashes the "unruly mob," whose irrational, destructive, and barbaric behavior is able to undermine civilization itself.

25. T/F* Psychoanalysis saw collective behavior as beneficial to the development of the individual personality.

26. The person most associated with psychoanalysis is
    a. Fritz Perls.
    b. Gustav Le Bon.
    c. Talcott Parsons.
    d. * Sigmund Freud.

27. One strain of psychoanalytic thinking explained the large attraction to fascist movements of the 1930s and 1940s as
    a. evidence of the Oedipal complex.
    b. indication of the society's addictive tendencies.
    c. *the mass response to the "authoritarian personality."
    d. a failure of the superego.

28. Mass society theory sees collective behavior as growing in response to
    a. the authoritarian personality.
    b. the lack of a class consciousness.
    c. * anomie and social disintegration associated with large-scale social change.
    d. the desire to foment revolution.

29. All of the following theories regard social change as the *cause* of problematic collective disruptions EXCEPT
    a. mass society theory.
    b. structural strain theory.
    c. crowd theory.
    d. *social transformative theory.

30. T*/F: Mass society theory argues that a stable society rests on strong class and group solidarities.

31. The theory of the underclass explains poverty as resulting from
    a. *improper attitudes, values, and behavior.
    b. blind allegiance to a charismatic leader.
    c. a lack of drive and desire.
    d. an adolescent-like rebellion against the status quo.

32. According to structural functionalism, social stability rests on all of the following EXCEPT
    a. the presence of a common set of values.
    b. *an autonomous leader able to make decisions rapidly.
    c. the proper integration of subsystems, each of which performs a different but necessary role in the larger system.
    d. the ability of societal structures and institutions to adapt to change.

33. T/F*: According to structural functionalism, a change in one part of the system has no affect on the other parts of the system.

34. Discussion Question: Abramovitz describes a "paradigmatic shift" occurring during the 1960s and 1970s that dramatically changed the study and understanding of collective behavior. What precipitated this paradigmatic shift? In what ways were the new social theories different from the classical theories?

    Answer: The 1960s and 1970s was a period of many social movements: the student movement, civil rights movement, antiwar movement, women's liberation movement and others. The dominant social movement theories nonetheless failed to anticipate or understand them. According to classical theories of social movements, collective behavior was spontaneous, irrational, and a noninstitutionalized response to abnormal conditions created by structural strain and social change. Yet these premises did not accurately describe the social movements of the 1960s and 1970s. The incongruity between theory and reality triggered a paradigmatic shift that dramatically changed the study and understanding of collective behavior.
    The major shifts between the classical theories of social movements and the new theories developed at this time were (1) the new theories rejected the view of social movements and their participants as irrational and deviant; (2) the decision to join a social movement was seen as a rational decision based on specific goals and a clear assessment of the costs and benefits of participation; and (3) the new theories did not denigrate pursuing social change outside of mainstream channels.

35. According to the rational crowd theory
    a.* the "crowd" was seen as a temporary gathering of people who shared a common

       focus of attention and who influenced one another.
     b. the behavior of crowds was always something to fear.
     c. crowds were seen as evidence of deviant behavior.
     d. all of the above.

36. Rational crowd theory defines certain civil disorders (riots) as
     a. examples of the crowd mindlessly following a manipulative leader.
     b. examples of irrational exuberance.
     c. * rational and adaptive responses to anger and oppression.
     d. gang mentality taken to the extreme.

37. Relative deprivation theory emerged, in part, to explain
     a. why the most deprived people engaged in collective behavior more often than better-off
        individuals and groups.
     b. why people in the same family who are poor often engage in collective action.
     c. * why the most deprived people engaged in collective behavior less frequently than
        better-off individuals and groups.
     d. none of the above.

38. Status strain theory argues that people join social movements when
     a. it becomes a status symbol to do so.
     b. * their symbolic position changes for the worse.
     c. they feel living conditions for the poor can no longer be tolerated.
     d. none of the above.

39. Which of the following is an example of social movement theorists turning to economic
     concepts to disprove the notions of irrationality and deviance built into classical
     collective behavior theories?
     a. crowd theory.
     b. structural functionalism.
     c. political opportunity structures theory.
     d. * rational choice theory.

40.T*/F: Rational choice theory presumes that individuals are autonomous reasoning beings
     whose decisions reflect narrow self-interest rather than common values and goals.

41. Discussion Question: What is the "free-rider" concept? Why is this concept important for
     social workers to understand? Do you agree with economist Mancur Olson's ideas about
     how to overcome the "free-rider" problem?

     Answer: According to rational choice theory, individuals make decisions based on their
     own individual self-interests, not those of the group or larger community. Free-rider
     theory argues that if an individual can benefit from the gains won by collective action or a

social movement without having to participate in the movement, then there is no rational reason for the individual to participate. Instead, the individual can be a "free-rider," that is, enjoy the benefits without paying the costs of participation.

As social workers, we need to understand the concept of the free-rider if we are to successfully mobilize individuals to fight for issues of economic and social justice. Economist Mancur Olson argued that to attract participants, organizations and social movements must offer special incentives to members and to those who participate in collective actions. Most trade unions and professional organizations follow this principle.

Others, however, dispute Olson's belief in the necessity of special incentives. They argue that thousands of people have joined movements to express solidarity and to fight for causes in which they believe very strongly. Radical feminists further this argument, contending that rational choice theory reflects a male bias in its analysis of why people do or do not participate in collective action. Women, they argue, may choose to participate in social movements because of empathy, a desire for connection, a sense of nurturance and a belief in interdependence, traits and beliefs not accounted for by rational choice theory.

42. A theory of social movements that draws heavily on Rational Choice Theory is
     a. crowd theory
     b. social strain theory
     c. relative deprivation
     d. * resource mobilization theory

43. Discussion Question: What is resource mobilization (RM) Theory? How does it differ from rational choice theory?

     Answer: Like rational choice, resource mobilization theory contends that individuals carefully assess the relative benefits and costs of any decision to be sure that the benefits outweigh the costs. Unlike rational choice theory, however, resource mobilization theory looks at social movement organizations, rather than individuals, as their center of analysis. RM theory views social movement organizations as rational institutions with centralized structures, clearly defined goals, bureaucratic control over resources, and measurable outcomes. RM theory argues that social movement organizations use the same deliberate and rational actions as individuals in making decisions, weighing relative benefits versus costs of political actions needed to maximize or defend their agenda.

44. T*/F: Resource mobilization theory normalized collective behavior as a rational means for solving social problems.

45. T*/F: Conflict theories of collective behavior gain popularity during periods of social upheaval.

46. Conflict theories differ from other theories of collective behavior because
    a. they are rooted in a Hobbesian notion of "man's war of all against all."
    b. *they view collective behavior in political rather than psychological or organizational terms.
    c. they focus on the increased tendency of modern humans to be aggressive.
    d. none of the above.

47. Resource Mobilization Theory is interested in
    a. * the conditions that promote the growth and political effectiveness of social movement organizations.
    b. the psychological factors that influence someone to join a social movement.
    c. how an individual assesses relative benefits likely to accrue from making a particular decision.
    d. how individuals respond to charismatic leaders.

48. T/F*: Resource mobilization theory concludes that the social movements of the 1960s were a result of the breakdown of the institutions of social control.

49. All of the following contributed to the growth of social movement organizations during the 1960s EXCEPT
    a. *the widespread hippie culture.
    b. an increased number of private foundations and religious organizations willing to fund reform causes.
    c. the availability of the media to devote more time to domestic social problems.
    d. the availability of individuals wanting to work as social movement organizers.

50. T*/F: Resource mobilization theory argues that social movement organizations are inherently more effective than informal, decentralized, less well-endowed groups.

51. Critics fault resource mobilization theory for all of the following EXCEPT
    a. downplaying social movements of the poor.
    b. dismissing the more unconventional mass politics that proliferated during the late 1960s and 1970s.
    c. ignoring questions of individual motivation and social interaction, as well as questions
        about the role of social structures.
    d. *not taking a rational approach to their analysis of social movements.

52. All of the following are true about political opportunity structures (POS) theory EXCEPT
    a. POS theory focuses on the changing features of the political environment that either encourage or discourage people from using collective action to secure social change
    b. *POS theory focuses on an organization's capacity to mobilize resources.

     c. POS theory links the possibility of social movement activity to the growth and transformation of the state.

     d. POS lays out the dimensions of the political system that make it more or less receptive to the demands of social movements.

53. Social movements stand a better chance of succeeding when the prevailing political conditions
     a. reveal potential allies.
     b. exacerbate the vulnerability of the authorities.
     c. lower the "costs" of collective action.
     d. * all of the above.

54. Discussion Question: Abramovitz identifies four types of political opportunity structures that, depending on the particular circumstances, may encourage or discourage people from using collective action to fight for social change. What are these opportunity structures?

    Answer: The four political opportunity structures Abramovitz identifies are:

    a. the relative weight and independence of the judicial, legislative, and executive branches in the government. For example, Abramovitz notes that because the United States has a strong, active, and relatively independent judiciary, social movements regularly use the judicial system and try to win their cases in court.

    b. the degree of cohesiveness among the governing authorities. If there are internal divisions within centers of decision-making, the ruling power of the elite may be undermined, creating an opportunity for organized challengers to push their agenda or even to topple those in power.

    c. a time when elected officials support and legitimize social movements in hopes of building or rebuilding their own popular support. Political leaders look for additional outside support when an economic decline, the endorsement of an unpopular policy, or other events cost them regular constituency support.

    d. the prevailing political climate: Is it one of openness or repression? During periods of openness, the political climate facilitates the emergence and success of a wide variety of social movements. During more repressive periods, the political climate often stymies or represses oppositional social movements.

55. Discussion Question: Drawing on the four political opportunity structures identified by Abramovitz, how would you assess the current political climate for using collective action to fight for social change? Explain your thinking.

56. T*/F: It is a truism that any door opened by political leaders may also be slammed shut.

57. T*/F: New social movement theory has as its base Western European social theory and political philosophy rather than American schools of sociology.

58. NSM theory makes all of the following arguments EXCEPT:
    a. Classical Marxism cannot explain post-industrial forms of collective behavior.
    b. *Modern technology makes more classical models obsolete.
    c. Classical Marxism is deficient because it focuses too exclusively on conflicts between labor and capital.
    d. The conditions of postindustrial society have undermined the old social movements and generated new social movements.

59. Which of the following contributed to the rise of NSM theory?
    a. the weakening of the labor movement due to globalization and the deindustrialization of the nation's central cities.
    b. the failure of unions to incorporate other economically exploited, excluded, and marginalized groups (e.g.,youth, women, people of color, unskilled workers) into their ranks.
    c. government's systematic attack on organized labor and welfare state benefits.
    d. * all of the above.

60. Discussion Question: What is the focus of NSM theory? In what ways does it build on Marxism? What means does NSM use to appeal to people from different classes, of varied identities, and with a wide range of grievances?

    Answer: NSM theory focuses on conflict surrounding both political and cultural domination. It builds on Marxism by including in its analysis

    a. the political conflicts associated with advanced capitalism.
    b. the class structure.
    c. the role of the state.

    NSM appeals to a wide variety of people through its emphasis on issues that go beyond economic oppression. For example, NSMs oppose cultural intrusions, oppressive discrimination, bureaucratic domination, unrestrained militarism, and environmental devastation.

61. All of the following are characteristics of NSMs EXCEPT
    a. local in organization and focus.
    b. antibureaucratic.
    c. * global in organization and focus.
    d. antihierarchical.

62. T/F*: NSMs envision a highly centralized, highly regulated society that will promote the equality of all.

63. T*/F: One of the main foci of NSMs is the cultural oppression that results from mainstream culture's control over such things as definitions of self-worth and overall way of life.

64. T*/F: NSMs agree with feminism that "the personal is political."

65. T*/F: The agenda of NSMs is one of emphasizing identity issues or identity politics.

66. Discussion Question: In what ways do the NSMs go about attempting to rescue ethnic, racial, gender, and other identities from their distortion or erasure by the dominant culture?

    Answer: NSMs attempt this task through several methods:

    a. working to help members of oppressed groups rid themselves of stereotypic ideas and beliefs that oppressed people, uncritically and unconsciously, often accept as true but that stand in the way of progress. Some examples include the internalization by blacks of white values and racist attitudes, the acceptance by women of their place in the home, and the guilt felt by homosexuals because they are not straight.

    b. expanding mainstream ideas of "normality." For example, the lesbian and gay movements in the 1960s and 1970s worked to depathologize homosexuality. In the 1980s, they worked to expand the perception of the movement from one of white, middle-class gays to one that included a wider range of sexually, economically, and racially marginalized groups. In a similar fashion, the movement of differently abled persons has worked to change traditional perceptions of disability as a sick, abnormal, and pathetic condition.

    c. using their collective power to undo homophobia, sexism, racism, or ableism to gain recognition, visibility, and dignity for the group.

67. T*/F: NSMs remind us that a society that has the power to produce contains within it the power to destroy.

68. T*/F: Social movements appear when subordinated groups decide that authorities have appropriated an unfair share of societal status, privilege, wealth, or power.

69. T/F*: NSM theories treat the concept of identity in a manner similar to strain theories and relative deprivation theory.

70. Critics of NSMs
    a. fear the focus on the politics of difference discourages oppressed groups from joining together.
    b. call for building coalitions, seeking a unified effort in the pursuit of justice for all.
    c.*both of the above.
    d. neither of the above.

71. Marxism includes
    a. a critique of bourgeois society.
    b. a historical analysis of exploitation.
    c. a vision of a more humane society.
    d. * all of the above.

72. T/F*: Much of twentieth-century social movement theorizing by mainstream social scientists endorses a Marxian analysis of capitalism and class conflict.

73. T*/F: Marxism is an example of a conflict theory.

74. Discussion Question: Marxist theory suggests that the historic shift from feudalism to a market economy uprooted masses of people and ushered in economic arrangements favoring the owners of private property over others. Discuss how the new class structure unequally distributed power and control between those who owned the means of production and those who were forced to sell their labor in exchange for wages. How did this distribution of power affect the working conditions of workers?

    Answer: Those who owned and controlled the means of production had greater resources, power, and control than those who earned their livelihood in factories and offices. The owners' profits came from paying workers as little as possible, demanding long hours of labor, rarely investing in improved working conditions, and excluding unions.

75. T*/F: Class conflict derives from the unequal class system created by capitalism.

76. T*/F: The leverage of workers in their struggle for improved wages and working conditions depended on the capitalists' reliance on labor.

77. The capacity of the working class to act politically depends on a social movement that includes
    a.   the emergence of organization.
    b. *the emergence of democracy.
    c.   the emergence of leadership and intellectual activity.
    d.   class consciousness.

78. Discussion Question: Discuss how the trade union movement evolved and advocated for

better wages and better working conditions.

Answer: Beginning in the 1820s, workers in the United States began to organize. The unions and workers' political parties that developed had a broad agenda calling for (1) equal and free universal education, (2) public lands for settlement, (3) restrictions on child and prison labor, (4) better working conditions for women, (5) the ten-hour day without a wage cut, (6) governmental control of the currency, (7) the right to organize workers, and (8) the creation of public works jobs for the unemployed.

Following the Civil War, the factory system employed more workers and exploitation intensified. As a result, in 1869, the Knights of Labor began and by 1886 claimed to have 700,000 members. In 1881, the American Federation of Labor (AFL) was formed to organize skilled white male workers. By 1892, the AFL had 250,000 members.

During the Great Depression of the 1930s, the industrial unions (auto workers, steel workers, etc.) joined forces to form the Congress of Industrial Organizations (CIO). This stronger labor movement successfully pressed the U.S. Congress to enact additional pro-labor laws, including (1) requiring employers to pay a minimum wage of $.25 per hour, (2) reducing the work week to 45 hours, and (3) outlawing labor by children under the age of 16.

The AFL and CIO merged in the 1950s to become the largest labor federation in the nation.

79. T*/F: The gendered nature of American society is so embedded in the culture and social institutions that its existence often goes unnoticed.

80. Socialist Feminism makes all of the following arguments EXCEPT
    a. *Women should not be required to work in the same labor contexts as men.
    b. There are conflicts that arise from the gendered structures of power in society.
    c. Tensions between men and women arise from the power imbalance that enables men as
       a group to dominate women as a group.
    d. Gender inequality is evident in the gendered division of labor that assigns men to the
       market (public sphere) and women to the home (private sphere).

81. T*/F: The focus of socialist feminists is class, patriarchy, and racial domination.

82. As a result of the first women's rights convention held in Seneca Falls, New York, in 1848,
    married women gained all of the following rights EXCEPT
    a. the right to own their own property.
    b. the right to keep their wages and inheritance.
    c. * the right to vote.
    d. the right to have joint custody of their children.

83. T/F*: From 1920 to the present, the women's movement has been a collaborative effort of white, middle class women, African American women, and Latino women.

84. Discussion Question: What role have poor and working-class women played in the women's movement? What issues have they mobilized around?

    Answer: Although the women's movement has largely been seen as a movement of white, middle-class women, this description does not tell the whole story. Women of color as well as poor and working-class women have organized at different times in history around those issues that most directly affected their lives. For example, at least since the early 1800s, low-income women have been involved in organized efforts to demand jobs, protest rising rents, and fight against the high cost of food staples. Black, working-class women formed housewives leagues in the 1930s and 1940s and launched "Don't Buy Where You Can't Work" campaigns. During the 1960s, low-income women became active in the war on poverty and the welfare rights movement.

85. The capacity of women to act politically to change gender inequality is dependent on all of the following *EXCEPT*
    a. the development of consciousness.
    b. leadership.
    c. organizational capacity.
    d. * educational achievement.

86. T*/F: Clubs, associations, alliances, and organizations formed by women created networks that became the infrastructure for collective action by women.

87. Which of the following helped fuel the first and second waves of feminism in the United States?
    a. women's shared experience of the denial of basic rights in society.
    b. women being deprived of control over their bodies.
    c. women being excluded from the centers of power.
    d. * all of the above.

88. T*/F: The structure and operation of racial domination created the conditions for collective actions among people of color.

89. T*/F: Racial formation refers to the process by which social, economic, and political forces determine the content and importance of racial categories.

90. T*/F: Racialization is the extension of racial meaning to a previously racially unclassified relationship, social practice, or group.

91. T/F*: Collective action by persons of color seeking greater access to societal resources began in the United States in the late 1800s.

92. People who opposed slavery and worked for its elimination were called
    a. liberators.
    b. equalists.
    c. *abolitionists.
    d. segregationists.

93. The oldest secular African American organization is
    a. the Urban League.
    b. the Rainbow Coalition.
    c. * the National Association of Colored Women.
    d. the Black Power Movement.

94. One of the central precipitating factors that helped to foster the labor, women's, and civil rights movements is
    a. * the clustering together of people.
    b. repressive actions by the government.
    c. increased belief in the "American way."
    d. none of the above.

95. Discussion Question: Discuss the factors that fueled the civil rights and black power movements.

    Answer: African Americans engaged in a historic conflict with the white power structure for a fair share of resources. Their exclusion from major economic and political institutions enabled some people of color to forge a powerful critique of racism and white supremacy.

96. T*/F: Ideology plays a major role in social movements seeking social change.

97. T/F*: Liberal social movements call for restoring tradition.

98. The major social movements in the United States including trade unions, civil rights, women's rights, gay rights, disability rights, welfare rights, the peace, environmental, antiwar, and antinuclear movements, all have which of the following in common:
    a. * They have accepted the capitalist economic system but have pressed government to compensate for its limitations.
    b. They have advocated for a complete overhaul of the capitalist economic system.
    c. They seek to limit the role of government.
    d. They demand transformative change.

99. T*/F: Reactionary social movements subscribe to an ideology of domination, obedience, and homogeneity.

100. T*/F: Radical social movements encourage struggles over control of scarce resources as a way to promote social change.

101. T*/F: Liberation movements aim to free people from certain beliefs and attitudes embedded in the dominant culture.

102. T*/F: The United States is the only Western democracy that has never elected a social democratic, socialist, or communist to national office.

103. Transnational globalization movements advocate for all of the following *EXCEPT*
    a. human rights.
    b. environmental concerns.
    c. the end of poverty, oppression, and collective violence.
    d. * increased free trade.

104. Discussion Question: For people to participate in social movements, the message of the movement must "make sense." Discuss the role of "collective action frames" in winning supporters, accumulating resources, and legitimating the cause of a social movement.

    Answer: Collective action frames are the messages created by social movements that give people a way to perceive the reality and severity of a social problem. Frames help to garner supporters by building on existing cultural narratives, tapping into local values, beliefs, and folk wisdom. Frames range from specific messages tied to the platform of a particular group or set of problems to generic master frames that cut across several organizations and movements.

105. Some examples of master frames are
    a. choice.
    b. rights.
    c. injustice.
    d. all of the above.

106. "Free social spaces" are"
    a. places in a community open to everyone.
    b. the necessary social distance between people seeking social change.
    c. locations where anarchists come together to advocate for anarchy.
    d. * places where people gather to talk things over and where ancient beliefs in inherited rights can be transmuted into collective action.

107. A well-known community organizer in the 1930s and 1940s who believed in emphasizing tactics and strategies over ideology and who believed that people banding together in neighborhood organizations could develop the power to meet their needs was
    a. Ted Kennedy
    b. * Saul Alinsky.
    c. Reverend Martin Luther King Jr.
    d. Reverend Al Sharpton.

Chapter 7

Social Welfare History in the United States

Summary: What is the meaning of social welfare history? How can the events of the past help us to understand social welfare policy today? This chapter addresses these questions and identifies certain themes that have persisted throughout the history of American social welfare. By the end of the chapter, students will have an understanding of the power and indelible nature of these themes and how, though centuries old, they still shape our thinking about many current social welfare policies.

Key Concepts: republicanism, less eligibility, social welfare, predestination, localism, poor houses, poor laws, worthy poor, unworthy poor, "farming out," outdoor relief, indoor relief, Industrial Revolution, abolitionism, monopolies, robber barons, "separate but equal" doctrine, social Darwinism, populism, Freedman's Bureau, Reconstruction, Charity Organization Societies, "friendly visitors," settlement house movement, Progressive Era, social reform, the New Deal, Social Security Act, Keynesian deficit spending, cold war liberalism, McCarthyism, the Great Society, the War on Poverty, globalization, market populism, federalism

Test Bank: The following questions have been designed to highlight the key concepts and ideas covered in this chapter. They may be used to test students' understanding of the material or to lead class discussions.

1. Discussion Question: As Americans, we know that every citizen is supposed to enjoy the right to vote. Yet an examination of American history indicates that this basic right of citizenship has not always been available to all. What historical and present-day examples raise questions about the universality of voting rights?

    Answer: There are a number of examples indicating that equal political rights have not always been available to all citizens:

    a. Until the 1840s, only white men who owned property could vote.
    b. Women were not granted the right to vote until 1920.
    c. In the South, law and custom worked to effectively disenfranchise African Americans until the Civil Rights Act of 1964.
    d. A congressional study found that in the presidential election of 2000, the votes of the poor and minorities were more than three times as likely to go uncounted as the votes of the more affluent.

2. T*/F: One of the myths that many Americans hold is that we are all middle class.

3. Blau argues that one of the central themes running through American history is
    a. the battle of the sexes.
    b. * the unrealized promise of equality for all

   c. the focus on the needs of the community, rather than on the needs of the individual.

   d. a belief in the importance of a strong central government.

4. T/F*: Historically, social welfare programs have been able to eliminate the inequalities produced by the larger political and economic system.

5. T*/F: In the early days of American history, the term "social welfare" meant simply direct aid to the poor.

6. Which of the following is a present-day example of a social welfare measure used to combat inequality?

   a. tuition assistance.

   b. affirmative action.

   c. job training.

   d. * all of the above.

7. Discussion Question: Blau identifies five policy traditions brought to the United States by English colonists. What are these five traditions?

   Answer: These are the five policy traditions:

   a. The first tradition had to do with popular perceptions of the poor. Drawing on Calvinism, this tradition stressed hard work as a divine vocation. Calvinists believed that if you worked hard and prospered, you would be rich. Conversely, if you were poor and suffered, it meant that you were predestined to be poor, and your poverty reflected your moral failings.

   b. Localism was the second British tradition adopted by the Americans. This tradition held local government responsible for the poor who lived within their jurisdiction. Local government was not responsible, however, for the poor from other areas.

   c. The third British social welfare tradition seeks to control the mobility of the labor force. If workers can get aid only in their own locality, they are forced to accept whatever jobs and wages are offered there. Limiting the mobility of the labor force kept taxes down and prevented workers from getting better-paying jobs in other communities.

   d. The fourth social welfare tradition inherited from the British was a reliance on institutions such as the poor house and the workhouse. This tradition allowed local government to tax property owners to care for the poor in their area and authorized local authorities to build "convenient houses of habitation."

e. The fifth British social welfare tradition is what has become known as "less eligibility." This tradition asserts that the recipient of relief is always supposed to have a lower standard of living than the lowest-paid laborer. The underlying belief is that no recipient of relief should have an incentive to "elect" to receive public benefits.

8. T*/F: American colonial governance enacted poor laws that closely followed on the British tradition.

9. The colonial economy was predominantly
   a. industrial.
   b. *agricultural.
   c. service-based.
   d. postindustrial.

10. T/F*: In contrast to the relative stability of the colonial cities, trade and wars could alter economic conditions in the rural areas enough to increase the number of impoverished people.

11. All of the following are characteristics of the South's economy from 1619 to 1783 EXCEPT
    a. a dependence on slave labor.
    b. * preindustrial and industrial businesses.
    c. agriculture that was centered around plantations.
    d. an absence of a large class of free laborers.

12. During colonial times, those people who received assistance were
    a. the sick and the aged.
    b. widows of sailors who never returned from the sea.
    c. unattached white women with children.
    d. * all of the above.

13. T*/F: During the colonial period, aid to healthy but poor male workers was rare.

14. Colonial politics focused on all of the following issues EXCEPT
    a. *equality of the races.
    b. relations with Britain.
    c. relations with the western settlements of each colony.
    d. local laws, including administration of poor laws.

15. The first rule of colonial poor law administration was
    a. to encourage new people to settle.
    b. to ensure that no one would go without.
    c. to negotiate positive relations with the indigenous populations.
    d. * to make poor people who did not already live there someone else's responsibility.

16. Discussion Question: During colonial times, an emerging republicanism was the prevailing ideology. What is republicanism? Whose interests does republicanism represent?

> Answer: Republicanism is an implicit belief that the individual has a fundamental sense of expanding political rights and economic possibilities. Republicanism represents the interests of white men who expect to benefit from their own hard work. This ideology did not recognize any circumstance in which an able-bodied man could not support his family.

17. Discussion Question: Colonial society also developed an ideology for and about women. Describe this ideology. Whose interests were represented by this ideology?

> Answer: The ideology that developed about women during colonial times asserted that families were economically productive units, and all members were important participants in the necessary work. Men were dominant in this ideology, ruling over a subordinate class of women, children, servants and slaves. Those white women who broke with this convention were classified with women of color as the "unworthy" poor.

18. T*/F: One of the ideologies about colonial society was that the hierarchy that existed between men and women was natural and normal.

19. Many of the social movements that developed during colonial times before the revolution were instigated by
    a. * the expanding class of free laborers.
    b. religious dissenters.
    c. ex-slaves.
    d. women.

20. T/F*: Just one social movement, the fight against "taxation without representation" led to the Revolutionary War and America's independence from Great Britain.

21. In colonial society, the issues that fueled most rebellions and uprisings were
    a. the lack of equal treatment of women.
    b. *hostility to the wealthy merchant class and slave rebellions.
    c. resistance to the military draft.
    d. racial injustice.

22. Discussion Question: Colonial society offered three primary means of relief for the poor. What were they?

    Answer:
    a. The first method of providing relief to the poor was "farming out," whereby the poor went to live with other families in town.

b. A second type of relief to the poor was called "outdoor relief" or relief in the family's own home. Outdoor relief included food, clothing, firewood, medical care, and sometimes a small weekly cash payment. This type of relief was offered most often to the sick, disabled, or old whites who conformed to definitions of the "deserving poor."

c. The third kind of assistance to the poor was known as "indoor relief." This was the preferred type of relief and required the poor to enter a workhouse, also known as an almshouse. The underlying belief of this type of aid was that putting poor people who were "less deserving" in an institution deterred others from deviating from the family ethic.

23. T/F*: The rise of indoor relief lessened the distinction between the "worthy" and "unworthy" poor.

24. All of the following are changes that occurred in the United States during the eighty-year period from the end of the Revolutionary War to the conclusion of the Civil War EXCEPT
   a. Production shifted from inside to outside the home.
   b. Production for domestic use shifted to production in factories.
   c. The beginning of the trade union movement.
   d. *The end of a plantation economy in the South.

25. T*/F: The period in U.S. history between the Revolutionary War and the Civil War can be characterized as a period of rapid change and tumult.

26. One of the central themes present during the time between the Revolutionary and Civil Wars was
   a. the beginning of the trade union movement.
   b. a turn toward institutions as a method of managing dependent people.
   c. a growing debate between the North and the South over the use of slave labor.
   d. * all of the above.

27. T*/F: During the period between the Revolutionary and Civil Wars, the first asylums for the mentally ill were constructed.

28. Discussion Question: Blau notes that during the period 1783-1865, the growth of asylums and workhouses reflected a desire for a return to a more stable social order and revealed the anxiety Americans were feeling about the changes occurring during this period. What were some of the economic changes going on during this period? What were some of the political changes? What were some ideological changes? What issues did the social movements of this time address? What were the historical themes of this era as they relate to the history of social welfare?

   Answer:
   a. Economic Changes: The period between 1783 and 1865 was when the Industrial Revolution began in America. Inventions like the spinning jenny, water frame, and

power loom helped to move production out of the home and into factories. The fabrication of products with interchangeable parts furthered this shift toward mass production. Railroads and new canal construction helped to make it possible to distribute goods at an affordable price. Labor for wages became more common, making workers increasingly interchangeable.

b. Political Changes: The debate over the issue of slavery was the dominant political issue of this time. This issue had a profound effect on all aspects of society, including the economy, trade, the settlement of the frontier, and social welfare.

c. Ideological Changes: Two related ideologies gained strength during these years. The first ideology combined a commitment to work for wages, upward mobility, abolitionism, devotion to the Union, and a desire to export the wage system to each new state. The second ideology was the industrial family ethic, an ideology that assigned the world of work to men and domesticity to women. Anyone who could not conform to the roles demanded by these ideologies risked stigmatization, a principle that came down especially hard on the poor.

d. Social Movements: The most significant social movements of this era focused on the issues of race, gender, and class. The abolitionist movement worked to eradicate slavery; the women's movement demanded the right to vote; and upper-class social reformers worked to improve the conditions of the poor.

e. Social Welfare History: During this era, the federal government disclaimed any responsibility for social welfare, so the burden for caring for the poor and disabled continued to fall on the states and the localities. Most charities, however, would not assist African Americans, so a number of organizations such as the Black Masons, the Negro Oddfellows, and the African Female Union were established to provide medical, educational, and burial services for the African American population. Dorothea Dix advocated to get the federal government to provide public lands on which to construct asylums for the mentally ill, but President Pierce vetoed this legislation because it would establish a precedent for other kinds of federal responsibility. The result was that social welfare remained a state responsibility until the 1930s and the advent of the New Deal.

29. Discussion Question: What were the two main issues involved in the debate about slavery? What were the implications of this debate for social welfare?

Answer: The first issue in the debate about slavery was the moral issue: How could one justify owning another human being? The second important issue related to slavery focused on what kind of a labor system America would have: Would it be one where employers owned their workers or one in which workers were ostensibly free because their employers paid them a wage? This question was particularly important during this era because of the American frontier, where new states were forming as their populations increased. Would these states be slave or free?

The debate over slavery had critical implications for social welfare. If the new states were to be slave states, then their economic system could not absorb the poor and the unemployed of the eastern cities, and the pressure for substantial social reforms in the East would intensify.

30. Discussion Question: The period between the Civil War and the Progressive Era, 1865-1900, was marked by many changes. What were some of the economic changes going on during this period? What were some of the political changes? What were some ideological changes? What issues did the social movements of this time address? What were the historical themes of this era as they relate to the history of social welfare?

Answer:

a. Economic Changes: During the period from 1865 to 1900, the U.S. economy shifted from one of small businesses to one of large businesses. Corporations first appeared and with them, the creation of near monopolies in many major industries. Measured by the quantity and value of its products, America became the first manufacturing nation in the world. This was the age of laissez-faire, of robber barons, and of largely unregulated capitalism. It was a period of boom and bust. During the bad economic times, banks closed, bankruptcies skyrocketed, millions of people lost their jobs, workers went on strike, and there were clashes between strikers and federal troops that resulted in the loss of many lives.

b. Political Changes: The Republican Party dominated politics for most of this period. They supported the vote for African Americans, helping to elect blacks to southern state legislatures, the U.S. Senate and the U.S. House of Representatives. This Republican-African American coalition enacted the Thirteenth, Fourteenth and Fifteenth Amendments to the Constitution, outlawing slavery, guaranteeing citizenship to everyone "born or naturalized in the United States," and extending the vote to all male citizens. In addition, because the U.S. government had not yet developed much of a bureaucracy, the power of the judiciary was especially important. The courts struck down most pro-labor legislation and were responsible for establishing the "separate but equal" racial doctrine.

c. Ideological Changes: The predominant ideology of the period was social Darwinism, which meshed with the need of the era to have an ideology that justified competition, declared the winners of the competition to have triumphed by right, and opposed any interference in economic and social affairs.

d. Social Movements: There were a number of social movements during this period. They included a labor movement in the cities of the Northeast and the Midwest, the rise of the Ku Klux Klan in the South, and a populist movement in the Midwest. Through acts of terror, the KKK worked to ensure that African Americans returned to the bottom rung of society. The populists, representing the interests of farmers, fought for a graduated income tax, an eight-hour day, and public ownership of major industries like the telegraph and the railroad.

e. Social Welfare History: The federal government established the Freedman's Bureau. For a brief time (1865-1872), it distributed food and shelter, opened thousands of schools for both black and white children, and offered land at a minimal cost to a predominantly African-American population. Social Darwinists fought against social reforms, arguing that coddling the poor with charity would lead to the "survival of the unfittest" and disrupt the social order. Yet this was also the era that witnessed the founding of the first Charity Organization Societies and the first settlement houses. In addition, just prior to the turn of the century, a few formal education programs began to train "professional" social workers.

31. The two "pillars" of the rising corporate order in the post-Civil War economy were
    a. high wages and generous social welfare benefits.
    b. low taxation and generous social welfare benefits.
    c. * cheap labor and even cheaper welfare.
    d. high wages and meager social welfare benefits.

32. The period directly after the end of the Civil War was known as
    a. the Progressive Era.
    b. the New Deal.
    c. the Great Society.
    d. * the era of Reconstruction.

33. The political party most associated with the South and the institution of slavery was
    a. * the Democratic Party.
    b. the Republican Party.
    c. the Tory Party.
    d. the Green Party.

34. Which of the following is TRUE of the post-Civil War era?
    a. Many progressive social reforms were enacted.
    b. * The politics of this period hindered social reforms at every level of government.
    c. The labor movement gained strength partly as a result of a number of favorable pro-labor decisions by the courts.
    d. Women gained the right to vote.

35. The Supreme Court in *Plessy v. Ferguson* (1896) established the doctrine of
    a. school integration.
    b. * "separate but equal."
    c. equal rights for women.
    d. public employees not being allowed to strike.

36. T/F*: Charles Darwin (1859) argued that the principle of "survival of the fittest" governed both animals and human beings.

37. The person most responsible for popularizing social Darwinism in the United States was
    a. John D. Rockefeller.
    b. Henry Clay.
    c. Charles Darwin.
    d. * William Graham Sumner.

38. Adherents of social Darwinism argued that
    a. competition was natural.
    b. the principle of "survival of the fittest" had the status of a scientific law.
    c. social reforms constituted a foolish attempt to meddle with the natural order.
    d. * all of the above.

39. T*/F: The Charity Organization Societies used "friendly visitors" to investigate poor families and claimed to bring scientific innovation to charity work.

40. T/F*: The Charity Organization Societies represented the liberal wing of the charity movement.

41. T*/F: Settlement House workers did not make the usual distinctions between the "worthy" and the "unworthy" poor.

42. Which principle did settlement house workers stress in an attempt to combat reactionary politics and social injustice?
    a. rationality.
    b. objectivity.
    c. democracy.
    d. * all of the above.

43. Blau notes that one of the most significant ways the settlement house movement was different from prior social welfare organizations was that
    a. * it gathered facts about the poor and used these facts to interpret the poor to other people.
    b. it was made up of volunteers from the working rather than the privileged classes.
    c. settlement house workers did not seek to reduce the gap between the rich and the poor.
    d. all of the above.

44. Discussion Question: The period between the Progressive Era and the New Deal, 1900-1932, is one marked by changes in all aspects of society. What were some of the economic changes during this period? What were some of the political changes? What were some ideological changes? What issues did the social movements of this time address? What were the historical themes of this era as they relate to the history of social welfare?

Answer:

a. Economic Changes: The economy of this period was marked by attempts to provide just enough supervision and regulation of corporations to prevent any restriction of competition that would be detrimental to the public. This era also marked the beginning of a "professional managerial class" composed of teachers, doctors, journalists, and administrators who carved out a place for themselves between business and workers.

b. Political Changes: Much of the politics of this era focused on "corruption," and to reformers, corruption was often synonymous with an ethnic political machine. Frightened by the prospect of a political machine with a working-class base, reformers sought to end immigrant domination of city politics. In addition, the Progressive Era was the first time that the structure of state government served to hamper social reform.

c. Ideological Changes: The ideology of the Progressive Era combined moralism and empirical analysis in equal measure. Fueled by moralistic principles, reformers and muckraking journalists sought to expose the terrible conditions under which the poor were forced to labor and tried to enact reforms. Female reformers highlighted women's unique capacity for caretaking and set out to preserve a separate domestic sphere for women. Progressives were also the first group of social reformers who actually ventured out to collect data about the poor.

d. Social Movements: Three social movements created the context within which many of the reforms of the Progressive Era took place: the rise of a radical left, the first national movement for black people, and the women's suffrage movement that won women the right to vote.

e. Social Welfare History: The Progressive Era was when social work crystallized as a profession. In response to the criticisms of Abraham Flexner, social work turned its focus from social reform to identification of the skills and knowledge base that social workers could claim as uniquely theirs.

45. Discussion Question: Most accounts of the Progressive Era stress the importance of its reforms. Blau, however, argues that as important as they were, these reforms do not warrant characterizing the Progressive Era as a time of fundamental change. What is the basis of Blau's argument?

Answer: Blau argues that even though there were many important reforms enacted during the Progressive Era, the reformer's agenda was "emphatically corporatist." While working to reduce the worst excesses of the industrial system, these reforms preserved its fundamental political and economic hierarchies.

46. T*/F: The Progressive Era was probably the twentieth century's low point in the treatment of African-Americans.

47. Discussion Question: What was the view of most reformers of the Progressive Era toward African Americans?

    Answer: Most reformers of this era assumed that African Americans were and should continue to be second-class citizens, restricted to menial jobs and denied the right to participate in the political life of the nation.

48. T*/F: During the Progressive Era, the Socialist Party gained strength and in the election of 1912, elected more than 1,200 members of their party to public office.

49. Which of the following are well known for their work in the settlement house movement?
    a. Carrie Nation and Betsy Ross.
    b. * Jane Addams and Lillian Wald.
    c. Lucretia Mott and Helen Caldicott.
    d. Gloria Steinem and Margaret Sanger.

50. The era during which social work crystallized as a profession was
    a. the Elizabethan Era.
    b. the Reagan Era.
    c. the Colonial Era.
    d. *the Progressive Era.

51. At the turn of the twentieth century, social work began to achieve "professional" status. Yet this status was not achieved without "cost." What was this cost?
    a. an agreement to focus more on politics and less on people's intrapsychic problems.
    b. an agreement never to compete with psychologists.
    c. * an agreement to minimize commitment to social reform.
    d. all of the above.

52. The person who questioned the right of social work to be seen as a profession was
    a. Mary Richmond.
    b. * Abraham Flexner.
    c. Jane Addams.
    d. Sigmund Freud.

53. The person responsible for seeking to distinguish the skills and knowledge base of trained social workers from the well-meaning efforts of volunteers was
    a. Eleanor Roosevelt.
    b. Susan B. Anthony.
    c. Dorothea Dix.
    d. * Mary Richmond.

54. T/F*: During the 1920's, the social work profession began to abandon its focus on psychoanalysis and turn, instead, to a focus on advocacy and empowerment.

55. Discussion Question: The stock market crash of 1929 and the Great Depression of the 1930s prompted a near collapse in many dimensions of American society.   The New Deal policies of President Franklin Roosevelt sought to pull the country back from the brink of disaster and restore stability. One of the best ways to understand the policies enacted during this era is to examine these changes. What were they? Following the policy model, can you list the economic, political, and ideological changes of this period? What issues did the social movements of this time address? What were the historical themes of this era as they relate to the history of social welfare?

    Answer:
    a. Economic Changes: The major economic event of the era was the stock market crash of 1929, followed by the Great Depression of the 1930s. Most stocks lost a substantial part of their value. As hundreds of thousands of workers lost their jobs, the unemployment rate reached 25 percent. The early New Deal policies of FDR were an attempt to restore the economy through programs designed to support corporations. Later New Deal policies (after 1935) changed focus and turned to social welfare legislation to put money in peoples' hands.

    b. Political Changes: The politics of social welfare in the New Deal accentuated the division between the state and federal governments. Even as the federal government enacted social welfare legislation to assist single mothers with children, the elderly, the disabled, and the unemployed, most programs granted individual states the power to determine benefit levels and/or eligibility criteria.

    c. Ideological Changes: The pursuit of greater inclusiveness was the dominant ideology of the New Deal. Since the old system had broken down, the success of any new system depended on granting political and economic rights to the working class and the poor. This new inclusiveness did not, however, seek to change the status of all groups. African Americans continued to be viewed as second-class citizens, and women continued to be seen as belonging in the home.

d. Social Movements: Many social movements arose in the 1930s, including those focused on helping people to secure food, shelter, and clothing; those fighting to establish trade unions; those fighting for benefits for the unemployed; those fighting for an old-age pension; and those representing business interests opposed to the New Deal.

e. Social Welfare History: Most historians view the New Deal as being made up of two distinct periods: the first in 1933-1935 and the second in 1935-1937. During the early period, the Roosevelt administration experimented with a host of programs designed to salvage the collapsing economy. These programs included the National Industrial Recovery Administration, the Federal Emergency Relief Administration, the Civilian Conservation Corps, the Civil Works Administration, and the Works Progress Administration. Most of these programs provided jobs for the unemployed, but the jobs were not permanent, and the program favored the employment of white men. During the second New Deal, the enactment of several pieces of landmark social legislation helped to create a more permanent safety net for the elderly, the poor, the disabled, and the unemployed. These included the Social Security Act, the Wagner Act, and the 1937 Housing Act.

56. T/F*: Keynesian deficit spending pulled America out of the Great Depression.

57. T*/F: If the Great Depression signified anything, it demonstrated the failure of an unregulated corporate system.

58. Two important goals of New Deal economics were
    a. * resurrecting the economy and keeping corporations profitable.
    b. encouraging savings and curbing consumer spending.
    c. encouraging stock market investment and equalizing the economic status of African-Americans and whites.
    d. all of the above.

59. Early New Deal policies (prior to 1935) could be characterized as a version of what economic policy approach?
    a. to the victor belong the spoils.
    b. compassionate conservatism.
    c. * trickle-down theory.
    d. none of the above.

60. Which statement best characterizes New Deal policies after 1935?
    a. * They tried to stimulate the economy through the enactment of social welfare legislation.
    b. They turned to corporations to lead the way out of the Depression.
    c. They relied on the economy to " correct" itself naturally.
    d. None of the above.

61. T*/F: The Social Security Act of 1935 established the modern American welfare state.

62. Discussion Question: Why were legislators from the South opposed to a single uniform standard of payment for recipients of Aid to Dependent Children (ADC)?

Answer: Southerners opposed a uniform standard of payment because it would have posed a two-pronged threat: first, a uniform standard of payment would have meant that blacks and whites were entitled to equal pay; second, that African American women working as field and domestic laborers would receive more money on welfare than from work at these low-paying, menial jobs.

63. T*/F: Until 1951, Social Security benefits were not available to domestic or agricultural workers.

64. T*/F: Concessions to "states' rights" weakened many New Deal policies.

65. One of the most significant and troublesome social welfare legacies of the New Deal was
     a. the universal nature of most of the benefits.
     b. the limited nature of the benefits that were offered.
     c. the generous amount of assistance earmarked for each needy individual.
     d. * the residual nature of most of the benefits.

66. All of the following groups were helped by New Deal legislation EXCEPT
     a. farmers.
     b. * African Americans.
     c. trade unions.
     d. the elderly, the poor, and the unemployed.

67. T/F*: The first minimum wage law was passed during the 1960s.

68. T*/F: The Liberty League was organized in the 1930s by several prominent corporate executives to resist "radicalism" and protect property rights.

69. Which of the following statements best describes the relationship between corporate America and the New Deal?
     a. Corporate America supported most of FDR's New Deal policies.
     b. Corporate America opposed most of FDR's New Deal policies.
     c. * Corporate America supported early New Deal policies, but opposed most of the later New Deal policies.
     d. Corporate America opposed early New Deal policies, but supported most of the later New Deal policies.

70. T/F*: Most of the programs enacted during the first part of the New Deal that provided jobs for the unemployed were focused on providing jobs for minorities and women.

71. T*/F: During the New Deal, many of the publicly funded programs that provided jobs had quotas on the number of racial minorities who could receive these jobs.

72. Eventually, the United States did pull out of the Great Depression of the 1930s, due mostly to
    a. the temporary public works programs that provided jobs for the unemployed.
    b. the social legislation of the second New Deal such as the Social Security Act and the Wagner Act.
    c. the implementation of Keynesian deficit spending economic policies.
    d. * the advent of World War II.

73. The Lanham Act of 1943 is important because
    a. it gave women equal rights.
    b. * it funded day care facilities so women could work while the men were off to war.
    c. it gave the government the right to round up and confine Japanese Americans in internment camps during World War II.
    d. it declared that segregation in schools must end and schools must desegregate.

74. One of the most important lessons for social workers to learn from the New Deal is
    a. *social welfare legislation frequently responds to the needs of the labor market.
    b. "make work" programs are the key to pulling the country out of a depression.
    c. mean-tested welfare programs are the most effective programs.
    d. during hard economic times, the country bands together and past racial and ethnic differences often disappear.

75. Discussion Question: The Cold War framed the period 1946-1968. The major economic, political, and ideological changes of the period, as well as social movements and social welfare history, must therefore be looked at within this context. What were some of the economic changes occurring during this period? What were some of the political changes? What were some ideological changes? What issues did the social movements of this time address? What were the historical themes of this era as they relate to the history of social welfare?

    Answer:
    a. Economic Changes: A distinguishing feature of this period of the twentieth century was that its income gains were broadly shared among all classes. Deficit spending on the part of government was the key to creating a widening prosperity. Most federal spending was devoted to military and social welfare purposes.

    b. Political Changes: During this post-New Deal era, the Democratic Party predominated, with the exception of the Eisenhower years 1952-1960. Until the antiwar movement rose in response to the Vietnam War, McCarthyism on the right and the civil rights movement on the left defined the contours of domestic politics.

c. Ideological Changes: Cold war liberalism was this era's dominant ideology. It assumed that a few well-chosen policies could preserve the private enterprise system. In the late 1950s, however, a "democratic left" began to challenge cold war liberalism. More liberal in its orientation, this ideology called for policies to promote racial equality, additional social programs to combat poverty, and the end of the arms race with the Soviet Union.

d. Social Movements: There were three great social movements of this period: the struggle for racial equality, the women's movement, and the opposition to the Vietnam War. The protests, demonstrations, boycotts, and actions by the leaders and supporters of these movements placed these issues on the national agenda and, in some cases, led to the enactment of significant legislation.

e. Social Welfare History: This era can be subdivided into three eras. The first, 1946-1953, was a time when conservatives fought against the continuation of New Deal policies. The second, 1954-1963, saw the growth of the civil rights movement and a shift from the McCarthyism of the early 1950s to a time of quickening social change. The third era, 1964-1968, was the era of the Great Society, the time when the assassination of President John F. Kennedy created the political momentum necessary to enact a number of key pieces of social legislation.

76. T*/F: Two of the biggest gains for workers during the 1950s were the corporate provision of pensions and health insurance.

77. T*/F: The use of deficit spending to create a well-functioning *peacetime* economy was used first during the post-World War II years.

78. The person most associated with the "Red Scare" of the early 1950s was
    a. President Dwight D. Eisenhower.
    b. Senator Ted Kennedy.
    c. Senator Jacob Javits.
    d. * Senator Joseph McCarthy.

79. T*/F: One of the effects of the anticommunism furor of the 1950s was the curtailment of the politics of social reform.

80. What major demographic shift between the 1930s and the 1960 put the southern wing of the Democratic Party in direct conflict with the northern wing of the Party?
    a. Large numbers of senior citizens moved from the Northeast to the South.
    b. * large numbers of African-Americans moved from the South to the North.
    c. large numbers of immigrants settled in the South.
    d. baby boomers moved from the South to the North.

81. Cold war liberals favored which policy?
    a. the use of Keynesian deficit spending to promote growth and prosperity.
    b. collective bargaining.
    c. a modest welfare state.
    d. * all of the above.

82. Michael Harrington's book The Other America, published in 1962, helped to explode which myth?
    a. that there is no such thing as elder abuse.
    b. that desegregated schools were better than segregated schools.
    c. * that poverty in the United States had been eliminated.
    d. that women who worked outside of the house were happier than those who were full-time homemakers.

83. T*/F: The modern civil rights movement dates from the *Brown vs. The Board of Education* decision in 1954.

84. The person whose refusal, in 1955, to give up her seat for a white man on a Montgomery, Alabama bus led to the desegregation of the entire bus system was
    a. Harriet Beecher Stowe.
    b. * Rosa Parks.
    c. Cicely Tyson.
    d. Sojourner Truth.

85. Discussion Question: Some social welfare historians of the civil rights movement have drawn a troubling conclusion about the use of violence. What is this conclusion and on what is it based?

    Answer: The conclusion of these historians is that while the early civil rights movement preached and practiced nonviolence, it appears that only the violent disruption of the status quo finally produced legislation granting the changes civil rights activists sought. They base this argument on the array of legislation and programs initiated after the rioting of the summer of 1964. These programs and legislation included the passage of the Civil Rights Act of 1964, the establishment of a federal Office of Economic Opportunity, the creation of the Head Start program, the development of the Job Corps program, and rising welfare payments in the inner city.

86. The person most associated with the Civil Rights Movement of the 1950s and 1960s is
    a. Stokely Carmichael.
    b. * Reverend Martin Luther King Jr.
    c. Langston Hughes.
    d. W. E. B. DuBois.

87. A key person in the development of the feminist movement of the 1960s was
    a. * Betty Friedan.
    b. Susan B. Anthony.
    c. bell hooks.
    d. Phyllis Schlafly.

88. The issues stressed in the early stages of second-wave feminism (1960s) included all of the
    following EXCEPT
    a. * voting rights for women.
    b. divorce law reform.
    c. equal pay for equal work.
    d. passage of the Equal Rights Amendment.

89. The Great Society and War on Poverty are both associated with
    a. * President Lyndon B. Johnson.
    b. President Dwight D. Eisenhower.
    c. President Richard M. Nixon.
    d. President Harry S. Truman.

90. The social work profession from the post-settlement house movement days
    until the early 1960s emphasized
    a. a community organization model to help communities give voice to their needs.
    b. a social advocacy model designed to identify the roots of inequality.
    c. * a casework model whose counseling orientation viewed the client's behavior apart
        from a social context.
    d. a "friendly visitor" orientation to help the poor adapt to the prevailing culture.

91. Discussion Question: Unlike some other periods, the time from 1969 to the present has been
characterized more by continuity than by change. Though this period has had both Republican
and Democratic presidents, policymakers from both parties believed that a reliance on the market
should power the economy. From this framework, examine the economic, political, and
ideological issues of the time, as well as the social movements and historical themes affecting
social welfare. What were some of the economic changes going on during this period? What
were some of the political changes? What were some ideological changes? What issues did the
social movements of this time address? What were the historical themes of this era as they relate
to the history of social welfare?

    Answer:

    a. Economic Changes: Mainstream economics returned to the belief that markets are self-
       adjusting and operate best with little interference. Five principles have guided
       economic policy: (1) globalization and free trade, (2) tax relief, (3) privatization

and deregulation, 4) labor flexibility, and (5) restraints on social welfare.

b. Political Changes: Two key political issues of this era have affected social welfare: the politics of taxes and the politics of race. Skilled at linking these two issues conservatives have forged a coalition of white middle- and working-class people angry about their inability to get ahead with those in the highest income brackets upset about their tax burden. The target of this coalition has been the social welfare system and African Americans deemed to constitute the largest percentage of welfare users. The other major political event of the era, the September 11, 2001 attack on the World Trade Center and the Pentagon, may have been responsible for the rise in favorable public attitudes toward government.

c. Ideological Changes: The era from 1969 to the present has been a fundamentally conservative period, though the type of conservatism taking center stage has varied from decade to decade: Nixon's standard republicanism for the 1970s, Reagan's social Darwinism for the 1980s, and "market populism" in the 1990s. While all of these ideologies share a belief in the market, each has adopted a somewhat different attitude toward social welfare. Nixon centralized power in the federal government and expanded social welfare; Reagan denounced the poor and contracted social welfare; and "market populism" lowered the profile of the poor while removing the issue of poverty from the public agenda.

d. Social Movements: Social movements of the past thirty-five years have had varying degrees of success in advancing their agendas. Some. like the women's movement and the civil rights movement, seem to have lost momentum; others, like the lesbian and gay movement have made substantial progress. In addition, an antiglobalization movement has arisen, giving hope for the development of an international social policy.

e. Social Welfare History: The history of social welfare during the past thirty years has been one of shrinking resources and social policy's subordination to the marketplace. Many social welfare programs have been transformed from a reliance on the public sector to a reliance on market forces. Job training programs have turned into workfare programs for welfare clients. Public housing programs have been slashed, health care has been reconceptualized as a market commodity for those who can afford it, and food programs have increasingly relied on the voluntary sector. As a result of these developments, the possibilities for an activist social welfare policy and an expansive social welfare practice have both shrunk.

92. The five principles guiding economic policy from 1969 to the present include all of the following EXCEPT
    a. globalization and free trade.
    b. *tighter regulation of multinational corporations.
    c. tax relief.

d. privatization and deregulation.

93. T*/F: The overarching principle governing economic policy from 1969 to the present is the belief that only the unimpeded market should establish a price for goods and services.

94. Which best describes the principle governing social welfare from 1969 to the present?
    a. Allow social welfare to grow in proportion to the growth of social welfare needs.
    b. Social welfare has no place in a market-based economy and therefore needs to be gradually phased out.
    c. * For the economy to grow, social welfare needs to be restrained.
    d. None of the above.

95. T/F*: The tax system from 1969 to the present, with the exception of the Clinton years, has become more progressive.

96. The term "labor flexibility" as used in the period since 1969 means
    a. employers should allow workers to have flexible work hours.
    b. workers need to be willing to change jobs and learn new skills if it is in the best interest of the company they work for.
    c. * workers need to be willing to accept lower wages and to give back benefits to help their employer compete in the global marketplace.
    d. students graduating from high school and college need to pursue those jobs and careers that will most enable the United States to keep the economy strong.

97. Discussion Question: What is the essence of the economic argument used today by those who object to social welfare spending? What are their objections to this type of expenditure?

    Answer: There are two economic arguments against social welfare spending. The first defines the issue as a matter of federal spending and objects to the government running a deficit. When the government runs a deficit, they argue, it competes with the private sector for capital and drives up the interest rate on borrowed funds. The second economic argument opposes social welfare expenditure because it disrupts the marketplace's natural capacity for price setting and requires employers to pay higher wages to attract a labor force.

98. Which president of the post 1969 era tried to legislate a national guaranteed income?
    a. * Richard Nixon.
    b. Ronald Reagan.
    c. Bill Clinton.
    d. George H. W. Bush.

99. The president responsible for establishing the Supplemental Security Income program (SSI) and the Comprehensive Employment Training Act (CETA) was
   a. Jimmy Carter.
   b. Dwight Eisenhower.
   c. Bill Clinton.
   d. *Richard Nixon.

100. What best describes Ronald Reagan's belief about the poor?
   a. The amount of money spent on them should be reduced, but they are still part of American society.
   b. * Poor people were seen as little more than a drain on the budget and as something less than full citizens.
   c. He ignored the poor and acted as if they did not exist.
   d. None of the above.

101. T*/F: Market populism believes that because social policy is market-based, it has little to do other than to privatize, deregulate, and ensure a healthy environment for business.

102. T*/F: At the beginning of the twenty-first century, both the civil rights movement and the women's movement have stopped functioning as organized social movements.

103. Discussion Question: What are the seven patterns that Blau identifies as central to U.S. social welfare history? Why is it important that we as social workers understand these patterns?

   Answer: Blau argues that these seven patterns define U.S. social welfare history:
   a. a belief that poverty is the fault of the individual.

   b. issues of race and gender pervade the history of U.S. social welfare, leading to policies that stigmatize and control people of color while defining women's roles in the context of the "family ethic."

   c. punitive social welfare policies enacted as part of a strategy of social discipline aimed at deterring poor people from relying on welfare.

   d. federalism has defined much of social welfare policy's evolution and in the process has often defeated policy development.

   e. progress in social welfare policy is reversible, meaning that at certain times, policies have been more generous and, at others, less generous.

   f. the state has always been involved in social welfare policy.

   g. the activity of the poor on their own behalf has been critical to progress in social welfare policy

It is important for us as social workers to appreciate these patterns in social welfare history both to recognize the factors that influence the formulation and promulgation of certain social welfare policies and to understand what may be impediments to good social work practice.

Chapter 8

Income Support: Programs and Policies

Summary: At the heart of the U.S. welfare state are income assistance programs. Yet there is much misunderstanding among the populace not only about the range of income support programs, but also about why they were instituted and who benefits from them. This chapter is intended to give students a working understanding of the breadth of these programs and how they work, as well as to shatter the misconception that income support programs assist only the poor. In addition, in this chapter and the four that follow, students are given a chance to see how the application of the policy analysis model put forth earlier in this text can be applied to pressing issues of public policy.

Key Concepts: income support programs, Social Security retirement, disability insurance, Supplemental Security Income, unemployment insurance, Temporary Assistance for Needy Families, Workers' Compensation, the Earned Income Tax Credit, general assistance, experimental Individual Development Accounts, Basic Income Grant, coentitlement, automatic disentitlement, unintended coentitlement, COLAs

Test Bank: The following questions have been designed to highlight the key concepts and ideas covered in this chapter. They may be used to test students' understanding of the material or to lead class discussions.

1. The term "coentitlement" means
   a. the number of benefits a person receives simultaneously.
   b. the only way to qualify for one entitlement is to qualify for another entitlement.
   c. that a person is receiving at least two entitlements.
   d. * the use of one benefit automatically entitles you to another.

2. Which of the following is a TRUE statement about income support programs in the United States
   a. There is only one large income support program in the United States
   b. * Some sources of income support will supplement one another, and others will conflict with one another.
   c. There is no stigma attached to receiving assistance from any income support program.
   d. Receiving assistance from one income support program automatically disqualifies you from receiving assistance from any other income assistance program.

3. Discussion Question: The author identifies four different social change mechanisms that prepared the way for passage of income support programs. What are the mechanisms he identifies? How did they contribute to the passage of income support programs?

   Answer: (see text for a complete description of social change mechanisms and how they led to specific income support programs).

The four social change mechanisms that the author identifies are:

a. An effort to stabilize the marketplace: this is linked to the development of the Workers' Compensation program.
b. Government structure and political control: this is linked the development of the Supplemental Security Income program.
c. Instability in the labor market: this can be linked to the development of the Earned Income Tax Credit.
d. An increase in social protest: this can be linked to the development of the Social Security Act.

4. Which factor does the author argue was the main trigger for the enactment of the Workers' Compensation program?
a. the injury and death of workers on the job.
b. the resulting poverty of families when workers were hurt on the job or died from their injuries.
c. * the instability in the marketplace caused by the flood of lawsuits filed when someone was injured or killed on the job.
d. the malnutrition suffered by children when the main breadwinner in the family was injured or killed on the job.

5. All of the following are TRUE statements about the Earned Income Tax Credit EXCEPT
a. *It helps to subsidize the income of all who earn less than $50,000 a year.
b. It helps to subsidize the income of low-wage workers.
c. It helps employers to keep labor costs down.
d. It means that taxpayers are essentially paying the bill for business's unwillingness to pay a decent wage

6. The theory of social unrest argues that
a. * the political and economic system depends on the silence of poor people.
b. most leaders of social movements and protests come from wealthy families.
c. the poor are usually excluded from social protest movements and demonstrations.
d. social protest usually results in more harm than good.

7. The Social Security Act was passed during whose presidency?
a. Dwight D. Eisenhower.
b. Woodrow Wilson.
c. * Franklin D. Roosevelt.
d. Lyndon B. Johnson.

8. The Social Security Act set up all of the following EXCEPT
a. Aid to Dependent Children (ADC).

b. retirement pensions.

c. * a guaranteed minimum income for everyone.

d. unemployment benefits for those who lost their jobs.

9. The late 1930s in the United States were marked by all of the following EXCEPT

a. a surge in union organizing.

b. * the passage of sweeping civil rights legislation.

c. mobilization for war.

d. continued social unrest.

10. The single largest social program in the United States is

a. unemployment insurance.

b. TANF (formerly AFDC).

c. SSI.

d. * Social Security retirement program.

11. Social Security is funded through

a. * payroll taxes charged to both employees and employers.

b. federal income taxes.

c. state sales taxes.

d. state income taxes.

12. Which is a TRUE statement about Social Security?

a. The Social Security tax is a progressive tax.

b. * Social security benefits are earning-related.

c. Poor women with children collect the most money from Social Security.

d. Social Security benefits do not include any cost-of-living increase.

13. A proposal favored by President George W. Bush with regard to Social Security is

a. have the system funded by state income taxes.

b. eliminate Social Security benefits for those with a net worth of over $1 million.

c. * privatize Social Security, thereby allowing individuals to invest the money themselves.

d. push the age at which individuals can begin receiving benefits back to 70.

14. Discussion Question: How are women shortchanged by the Social Security system? Why is this the case?

Answer: Because the Social Security system was set up at a time when most women did not work outside of the home, and this work was not valued as much as men's work, the system does not regard women as equal partners with men in the payment of benefits. Therefore, on retirement, a man receives 100 percent of his benefit, but his wife is entitled to no more than 50 percent of her husband's benefit. In addition, women who divorced after less than 10 years of marriage are not entitled to survivor insurance.

15. Many are concerned that the Social Security system will run out of money because
    a. the money has been invested in the stock market, which is not doing well.
    b. senior citizens have lobbied successfully to get their benefits increased
        every year.
    c. the younger generation is not as interested in making a lot of money so that the amount
        of money coming into the system is decreasing each year.
    d. * the ratio of workers to beneficiaries is dropping precipitously.

16. Discussion Question: What is the difference between SSI (Supplemental Security Income)
    and SSDI (Social Security Disability Insurance)?

    Answer: Unlike SSDI, which is a form of social insurance for workers who are unable to
    engage in "substantial gainful activity," SSI is a federal means-tested income support
    program for the aged, blind and disabled. SSI is not a form of social insurance, but a
    welfare program for poor individuals who are also aged, blind, or disabled and are not
    disabled solely because of alcohol or drug addiction.

17. Discussion Question: The author points out that SSI embodies the contradictions of the
    welfare system in the United States. Explain.

    Answer: Even though those who are entitled to receive SSI are regarded as the "worthy
    poor" (the aged, blind, and disabled), in part because they are unable to work through no
    fault of their own, still SSI is a means-tested program with difficult eligibility
    requirements and low monthly benefits.

18. Discussion Question: This chapter notes that since its inception in 1997, TANF has
    succeeded in reducing welfare caseloads anywhere from 57 percent to more than 90
    percent. On this basis, can we say that the program is an unqualified success? Why or
    why not?

    Answer: Many point to the dramatic drop in the welfare caseloads and use this reduction
    as a measure of the program's success. Others judge the program a success because of
    studies showing that almost half of those who left the welfare rolls are working. Yet
    critics of the reforms enacted under TANF argue that the economic boom of the late
    1990s may account for up to 44 percent of the drop in welfare caseloads. Additionally,
    critics cite the failure of many states to create sufficient day care to care for the children
    of the women forced to return to work. Most important, critics ask whether TANF was
    created to get people off welfare or to end poverty.

19. Discussion Question: President George W. Bush has proposed an expansion of the work requirement under TANF from 30 hours per week to 40 hours per week. Do you think this proposed policy change is a good one? Why or why not?

> Answer: Critics of this proposal for an expanded work requirement point to the lack of adequate day care options for mothers who must work to receive their TANF benefits. They worry also that to create the additional make-work programs to accommodate individuals who must work 40 hours per week, states may choose to divert money from day care to fund these additional jobs.
> Proponents of the Bush legislation trace the success of the 1996 welfare reform to its insistence on work. They reason that if 30 hours a week had a positive effect on poor peoples' work ethic, 40 hours a week will be even more beneficial.

20. Discussion Question: The Bush administration's TANF reauthorization proposal contains provisions that are designed to encourage single mothers receiving benefits to get married. What are the arguments made by those in favor of this proposal? What are the arguments of those opposed? What do you think about this proposal? What effect might this push for marriage have on your clients?

> Answer: Those who believe that poor women would be better off married point to the fact that if these women were to marry they would have someone with whom to share the costs of housing, food, and so on,. and in this way might be more likely to raise themselves up out of poverty. In addition, conservatives argue that two-parent households are needed to do a proper job of child rearing. Critics of this emphasis on marriage note that women who are poor are not necessarily going to meet a man able to earn enough to change the economic situation of their family. In addition, as many as 30 percent of women on welfare report that the men with whom they were involved were abusive. Is it good public policy to encourage women to go from economic dependence on government benefits to economic dependence on another person, rather than becoming economically independent?

21. Discussion Question: This chapter stresses that most studies of TANF have found two distinct groups of recipients who have left welfare. Describe these two groups.

> Answer: The first group identified by follow-up studies are those families who, in spite of leaving the welfare rolls to take full-time, year-round employment, experienced one or more serious hardships, such as going without food, shelter, or necessary medical care. The second group identified are those who earn about $7 an hour, work intermittently, and earn less than $10,000 a year. These are seen as welfare reform's "successes," even though they do not earn enough to provide the basic necessities for their family.

22. According to the author, perhaps the most striking outcome of welfare reform has been
    a. many individuals formerly on welfare are now enrolled in college programs.

    b. * a decline in the standard of living for former welfare families, even though the head of the household is now working.

    c. a decrease in homelessness and the use of food pantries and soup kitchens.

    d. all of the above.

23. This chapter emphasizes that the most important question with regard to welfare reform is

    a. how many welfare mothers are now back in the workforce?

    b. has the rate of marriage for welfare mothers increased?

    c. are welfare mothers having fewer out-of-wedlock children?

    d. * do the wages and benefits welfare mothers receive when they go to work actually improve their lives?

24. All of the following are TRUE about the Workers' Compensation program EXCEPT

    a. The program does not cover domestic and agricultural workers.

    b. Each state has its own program.

    c. Payments for injuries or disabilities can be time limited.

    d. * Payments for injuries or disabilities are means-tested.

25. The most effective program against childhood poverty in the U.S. is

    a. * the Earned Income Tax Credit.

    b. TANF.

    c. Head Start

    d. Child Health Plus.

26. All of the following are criticisms that have been leveled at the Earned Income Tax Credit program EXCEPT

    a. By subsidizing low-wage employees, there is less pressure on their employers to pay higher salaries.

    b. The program helps only the working poor and does nothing for the unemployed poor.

    c. * The program takes jobs away from those who truly need them.

    d. The program does not provide additional monies to families with more than two children.

27. All of the following are TRUE about general assistance programs EXCEPT

    a. * They are not means-tested programs.

    b. They are for individuals in need under age 65 who do not qualify for other assistance.

    c. They are locally administered and locally financed.

    d. These programs are optional and not all states offer them.

28. All of the following are TRUE about Individual Development Accounts (IDAs) EXCEPT

    a. They are about assets, not income.

    b. *These funds can be used by individuals only when they reach age 59.

    c. Under most IDA programs, the government matches savings by the poor.

    d. IDAs represent a widespread disenchantment with the ineffectiveness of income-based antipoverty programs.

29. Some policy experts criticize Individual Development Accounts (IDAs) because
    a. they give special treatment to the poor.
    b. most poor people do not know how to handle money.
    c. * they take the focus off of the structural origins of poverty.
    d. all of the above.

30. Proponents of instituting a Basic Income Grant (BIG) program argue that
    a. it could lead to the elimination of other costly income support programs.
    b. it would ensure everyone a minimally decent standard of living.
    c. it would be most beneficial to the poor.
    d. *all of the above.

31. T*/F: The Earned Income Tax Credit appealed to both liberals and conservatives.

32. T*/F: The Earned Income Tax Credit helped to manage the transition of the U.S. economy from a manufacturing to a service economy.

33. T/F*: Looking at the history of social welfare programs in the United States, it is clear that need alone is the factor that most often leads to the initiation of new income support programs.

34. T*/F: Most people receiving TANF are limited to a five-year lifetime cap on benefits.

35. T*/F: The Social Security Program includes both an old-age pension and disability insurance.

36. T*/F: Individuals who are self-employed pay twice as much Social Security tax as do individuals who work for others.

37. T/F*: The disability insurance provided under Social Security is a means-tested entitlement

38. T*/F: Proponents of Individual Development Accounts (IDAs) argue that the government offers tax breaks to the rich and middle class through individual retirement accounts, so the poor should also be offered some assistance.

Using the Policy Analysis Model

A great strength of this text is the introduction of a policy analysis model that students can easily learn to use. By looking at policies through the lens of economics, politics, ideology, social movements, and history, students can better understand not only how and why policies are formulated in a particular manner, but also who benefits from conceptualizing and implementing them in this particular way. In addition, students can see how policies have evolved over time and get a sense of the historical context in which they were created.

The following questions are proposed as a guide to help students analyze income support programs and policies from the perspective of the model's five conceptual areas.

39. Looking at income support programs through the lens of economics, what do we learn? What are the economic functions of income support programs?

40. Looking at income support programs through the lens of politics, what do we learn? What are the political functions of income support programs? What political issues are embedded in income support policies?

41. Looking at income support programs through the lens of ideology, what do we learn? What are the ideological underpinnings of income support programs? Who benefits from the reinforcement of these ideological ideals?

42. Looking at income support programs through the lens of social movements, what do we learn? What role have social movements played in the development of income support programs?

43. Looking at income support programs through the lens of history, what do we learn? What has been our historical experience about the development of income support programs? Have there been particular "historical moments" that provided the right context for the development of these programs? Have there been different historical stages that mark the development of income support programs?

Chapter 9

Jobs and Job Training: Programs and Policies

Summary: Closely tied to poverty, and residual in its orientation, employment policy has focused primarily on training the poor and unemployment. The Clinton administration tried to consolidate the 125 programs for this population in a new Workforce Investment Act. But because the Act retains separate funding streams for most of the major programs, it may not be able to bring about the desired consolidation or improve on what are, at best, the modest successes of job training. And although for the first time since 1981, there are some possibilities for public employment training, the United States, unlike most European countries, has never committed itself to a full employment policy.

Key Concepts: manufacturing sector, service sector, the Workforce Investment Act, adult employment services, dislocated workers, NAFTA-Transitional Adjustment Assistance Program, Job Corps, the National Farm Workers Job Program, Disabled Veterans' Outreach Program, Comprehensive Employment Training Program (CETA), Welfare-to-Work Program

Test Bank: The following questions have been designed to highlight the key concepts and ideas covered in this chapter. They may be used to test students' understanding of the material or to lead class discussions.

1. Employment training programs in the United States have been criticized for all of the following EXCEPT
   a. having too few slots available.
   b. *giving men priority over women.
   c. having training periods that are too short.
   d. for the most part, paying salaries that barely exceed the poverty level.

2. Most Americans today work in
   a. the manufacturing sector.
   b. agriculture.
   c. * the service sector.
   d. none of the above.

3. Discussion Question: Blau identifies five "triggers" that have brought about new federal job programs. What are these "triggers" and how have they worked to change employment policy?

   Answer: The five triggers Blau identifies are the following:

   a. policy-makers believing that employment training is important to upgrade the work force and to make the United States more competitive in the global market.

    b. a concern on the part of policymakers about issues of poverty and the structural impediments that make it impossible for the poor to advance.

    c. as a means to prevent social unrest among inner city youth.

    d. a desire to pass controversial legislation and using employment programs as the "payoff" for the support of unions.

    e. during periods of high unemployment or rapid transformation of the labor market where the obstacles to finding a job are so great that the federal government must create jobs.

4. On-the-job training programs are best suited to
    a. workers whose skills are outdated.
    b. workers ready to find a new job.
    c. individuals who have never worked before.
    d. *workers who need particular skills for a particular job in a particular type of company.

5. The Workforce Investment Act (WIA) provides all of the following EXCEPT
    a. * subsidized employment for a two year period.
    b. help looking for a job.
    c. assessment and case management to help individuals find jobs.
    d. job training.

6. The Work Investment Act (WIA) has been criticized for
    a. * providing job training only as a last resort.
    b. not targeting the hard-core unemployed.
    c. putting the bulk of the money toward jobs for youth rather than adults.
    d. not offering any services to the broader population.

7. The five main principles shaping the development of the Workforce Investment Act (WIA) include all of the following EXCEPT
    a. "Work First."
    b. increased reliance on market mechanisms.
    c. increased accountability.
    d. * narrowing the provision of services to fewer people in need.

8. The Workforce Investment Act (WIA) includes all of the following programs EXCEPT
    a. assistance to dislocated workers.
    b. adult services.
    c. *assistance to recent immigrants.
    d. youth employment programs.

9. A major cause of the economic problems in Native-American communities is
    a. the boom and bust cycles of the U.S. economy.
    b. * lack of investment in Native American communities.
    c. a lack of interest among Native Americans in developing businesses.
    d. all of the above.

10. One group of workers eligible to receive short-term cash assistance as well as employment education and training services is
    a. Native Americans.
    b. welfare mothers.
    c. youth who have droppped out of high school.
    d. * migrant and seasonal farm workers.

11. Critics of U.S. employment programs most often cite
    a. the large number of illegal immigrants who are able to access programs and services.
    b. * the lack of a single controlling authority and the degree of decentralization of the programs.
    c. the overemphasis on job development at the expense of training.
    d. the degree to which federally supported job programs have undermined the flow of the market economy.

12. Discussion Question: The author argues that linking public job creation to the issues of welfare and poverty will probably guarantee the demise of this program. Do you agree? Why or why not?

    Answer: Public job creation programs have often been criticized as "make-work." In the past, the linkage of this criticism with the stigma of welfare and poverty has usually undercut support for the program and led to its demise.

13. T/F*: Employment policy in the United States is very similar to employment policy in European countries.

14. T*/F: Most federal job programs offer training, but no job.

15. T*/F: In the mid-1990s, the federal government funded over one hundred different employment programs, but did not have a comprehensive employment policy.

16. T/F*: In the United States, the government has never expended money for the creation of public sector jobs.

17. T*/F: Despite claims to the contrary, the Workforce Investment Act (WIA) does not unify the nation's employment programs.

18. T*/F: Workers adversely affected by foreign trade are eligible for federal employment services such as career counseling and job placement assistance.

19. T*/F: The Job Corps is the largest education and job-training program available for youth in the United States.

20. T*/F: Youth employment services, though mostly for poor youth, also are open to high school dropouts, offenders, and pregnant and parenting teens.

Using the Policy Analysis Model

This section is designed to give students the opportunity to use the policy analysis model presented in this text to gain a fuller understanding of U.S. employment policies and programs and the issues and values underlying them. The questions that follow are proposed as a guide to help students as they try their hands at analyzing these policies from the perspective of the model's five conceptual areas: economics, politics, ideology, social movements, and history.

21. Looking at employment and training programs through the lens of economics, what do we learn? What are the economic functions of employment and training programs?

22. Looking at employment and training programs through the lens of politics, what do we learn? What are the political functions of employment and training programs? What political issues are embedded in employment and training policies?

23. Looking at employment and training programs through the lens of ideology, what do we learn? What are the ideological underpinnings of employment and training programs? Who benefits from the reinforcement of these ideological ideals?

24. Looking at employment and training programs through the lens of social movements, what do we learn? What role have social movements played in the development of employment and training programs?

25. Looking at employment and training programs through the lens of history, what do we learn? What has been our historical experience with regard to the development of employment and training programs? Have there been particular "historical moments" that provided the right context for the development of these programs? Have there been different historical stages marking the development of employment and training programs?

Chapter 10

Housing: Programs and Policies

Summary: The previous two chapters have discussed programs that operate on the demand side of the economic equation. This chapter, however, addresses one of the major items on which people spend money: housing. Spiraling housing costs, gentrification, real estate speculation, high construction costs and the withdrawal of the federal government from the housing market have all contributed to an increase in homelessness, as well as a great inequity in home ownership between whites and people of color. In addition, these factors have created a dichotomy in the housing market where the poor and working poor are increasingly unable to afford decent and safe housing, while the middle and upper classes garner a disproportionate share of the available housing stock.

      This chapter is intended to give students a comprehensive overview of U.S. housing policy and programs, as well as to describe the ways these policies and programs succeed and do not succeed in addressing the shortage of safe, affordable housing in this country. The chapter also challenges students' beliefs that the benefits of housing policy accrue mainly to the poor.

      At the conclusion of the chapter, students are given a chance to see how the application of the policy analysis model described in this text can be used to analyze a problem such as homelessness, thereby helping them to gain a fuller understanding of how and why current housing policies have not adequately addressed this issue.

Key Concepts: housing vouchers, Section 8, tax expenditures, homeownership, national minimum housing wage, housing affordability gap, homelessness, the suburbs, Housing Act of 1937, Housing Act of 1949, Fannie Mae, Freddie Mac, urban renewal, gentrification, Quality Housing and Work Responsibility Act of 1998, SROs, Low Income Housing Credit, public housing authority, National Tenants Union

Test Bank: The following questions have been designed to highlight the key concepts and ideas covered in this chapter. They may be used to test students' understanding of the material or to lead class discussions

1. All of the following have contributed to the decline in affordable housing stock EXCEPT:
      a. lack of space in older cities.
      b. gentrification.
      c. the increased cost of new housing construction.
      d. * the large increase in the Section 8 housing program.

2. The percentage of American households receiving direct housing assistance from the federal government has never been more than
      a. * 6 percent.
      b. 25 percent.
      c. 50 percent.
      d. 80 percent.

3. Which of the following is a TRUE statement about the U.S. housing policy?
    a. * U.S. housing policy is largely market-based.
    b. U.S. housing policy offers housing subsidies only to the poor
    c. U.S. housing policy is based on the assumption that most people cannot buy or rent housing on their own.
    d. U.S. housing policy relies on federal programs that use taxpayer dollars to build affordable housing for the poor and working poor.

4. Discussion Question: The author identifies three principles around which American housing policy is developed. What are they?

    Answer: The three principles the author identifies as central to U.S. housing policy are as follows:

    a. housing policy is rooted in the market.
    b. housing policy benefits banks, landlords and developers.
    c. housing policy gives more help to the wealthy than to the poor.

5. Discussion Question: The author identifies two "hidden" housing subsidies that disproportionately benefit the middle and upper classes. What are these subsidies? How do they disproportionately benefit the middle and upper classes?

    Answer: There are two "hidden" subsidies that greatly benefit anyone able to afford home ownership:

    a. the ability to deduct local property taxes from one's federal tax obligation
    b. the ability to deduct mortgage interest from one's federal tax obligation

    These subsidies disproportionately benefit the middle and upper classes because many more middle- and upper-class people can afford to buy homes than can the poor or the working poor.

6. An important feature of U.S. housing policy the author identifies is
    a. decreasing the number of people living in poverty.
    b. * increasing the personal wealth of American families.
    c. eliminating racism.
    d. eliminating all homeless shelters.

7. Discussion Question: The author states that home ownership rates mirror divisions of race and class. Explain.

Answer: A glance at the statistics about who can afford to buy a home in the United States suggests the clear racial and class differences. For example, 86 percent of households in the top quarter of income own their own home, compared to 48 percent of those in the bottom quarter of income. Looking at race, we see that home ownership rates for whites in 2002 equaled 74 percent, while for blacks the rate of home ownership was only 48 percent, and for Hispanics was just 47 percent.

8. Discussion Question: The author states that looking at home ownership data alone paints a false picture of the U.S. housing market. What data does he cite to support his assertion?

Answer: One example of the data presented by the author is that while the percentage of Americans able to afford their own home is higher than in many other industrialized nations, there are still many households who suffer from serious housing problems. For example, those earning a minimum wage in seventy U.S. metropolitan areas would have to work *one hundred hours per week* to pay for an apartment at the "fair market rent."

9. Discussion Question: Blau argues that public poverty (for example, homelessness) creates an ideological problem for the American sociopolitical-economic system. What does the author mean by this statement?

Answer: If instances of public poverty are seen as having structural causes, then the American sociopolitical-economic system is called into question: if homelessness is a result of the lack of affordable housing, then why doesn't U.S. social policy provide the means to create sufficient housing? But if public poverty can be attributed to the defectiveness of individuals, for example, alcoholism, drug addiction, or mental illness, then problems such as homelessness do not challenge the underpinnings of the American sociopolitical-economic system.

10. Conservatives argue that all of the following have contributed to the rise in homelessness EXCEPT
   a. individual deficiencies.
   b. single motherhood.
   c. the discharging of patients from mental hospitals.
   d. * a decline in wages.

11. Progressives argue that all of the following have contributed to the rise in homelessness EXCEPT
   a. the housing shortage.
   b. *the permissive social atmosphere that we have today.
   c. cutbacks in social welfare.
   d. a decline in wages, especially among low-paid workers.

12. Critics of the U.S. response to increased homelessness argue that
    a. increasing the number of shelter beds does not address the root causes of homelessness.
    b. criminalizing the behavior of homeless people does not address the problem.
    c. U.S. social policy has not addressed the real economic issues contributing to
        homelessness.
    d. * all of the above.

13. Discussion Question: How has housing policy in the United States been entangled with the
    issue of race? What has been the impact of this entanglement on African Americans and
    other people of color?

    Answer: Racial segregation has been a part of U.S. housing policy for a very long time.
    Until the passage of the Civil Rights Act of 1964, it was automatically assumed that
    blacks and whites would live in separate neighborhoods, where racial covenants
    frequently forbid the sale, rental, or use of homes by any nonwhite person. In addition,
    the restriction of public housing to poor people combined with racial discrimination to
    deny other housing options for people of color. As a result, large numbers of African
    Americans were relegated to public housing in inner cities.

14. All of the following are effects of housing discrimination EXCEPT
    a. greater concentrations of poverty in particular areas.
    b. a significant difference in home ownership rates between whites and people of color.
    c. * successful court challenges to the Civil Rights Act of 1964.
    d. poorer schools in areas populated predominantly by people of color.

15. Discussion Question: What "triggers" does the author identify as promoting change in
    housing policy? Are there different "triggers" when we talk about changing housing
    policy for the poor?

    Answer: The author identifies a number of triggers of change in housing policy. These
    include the following:

    a. a change in the prime interest rate set by the Federal Reserve Board. A rise in the rate
       makes it more difficult for a typical family to purchase a home, while lowering the rate
       makes home ownership more widely affordable.

    b. concern for a particular category of people—for example, World War II veterans—and
       wanting to make housing affordable for this group.

    c. economic considerations—for example, the desire to develop the suburbs.
       With regard to changes in housing policy for the poor, there are both similar and

different triggers. *Similar triggers* include a desire to make housing more affordable.

Different triggers include:

a. the degree of visibility of the problems of the poor—for example, crime, riots, and the spread of homelessness.

b. the perceived need for urban renewal.

16. Discussion Question: The author states that private poverty in the United States is usually acceptable as long as it is hidden. What evidence do you see that either supports or challenges the author's view?

Answer: Although it is true that some people may have feelings about "welfare mothers," the United States has relatively high poverty rates, and private poverty is widely accepted. Direct, unmediated encounters with public poverty—street beggars or customers using food stamps in a supermarket check-out line—typically arouse much strong stronger feelings.

17. Which of the following is the common thread shared by all "triggers" of change in housing policy?
   a. * a recognition that the living conditions of the poor alone do not bring about a change in housing policy.
   b. a desire to combat racial discrimination.
   c. a desire to even the economic "playing field" between those who have and those who do not.
   d. a desire to increase the number of nonwhites living in the suburbs.

18. The author argues that, in general, social change happens when
   a. social unrest threatens political stability.
   b. the economic interests of those in power are affected or threatened.
   c. the presidency passes from one party to the other.
   d. * a and b.

19. T/F*: During the past decade, the federal government has taken a much more active role in providing direct assistance to families unable to afford safe and decent housing.

20. T*/F: U.S. housing policy has many purposes other than the provision of housing.

21. T*/F: Before 1970, the homeless population in America consisted mainly of single, alcoholic men living in cheap single-room occupancy hotels in rundown areas of cities.

22. T*/F: The "new" homeless population includes families, youth and single women as well as single men

23. T/F*: Since the passage of the Civil Rights Act of 1964, housing discrimination has all but disappeared.

24. Discussion Question: The author identifies urban renewal and gentrification as two triggers of change in housing policy. What is your view of these policies? Explain. In what ways have your clients been affected by these policies?

25. Class Exercise: The author describes a wide variety of housing programs, each designed address the housing needs of a particular group or to support innovative approaches to dealing with the national housing shortage. One way to cover this material is to divide the class into small groups and assign each group one housing program that they must "market" to the rest of the class. The underlying premise is that there is a limited amount of money available to fund housing programs, and only those the class deems most worthy will receive funding. Key questions to be addressed by each group include the following:

   a. What is the purpose of the program?
   b. What group is the program trying to help?
   c. How does the program work?
   d. Who is likely to benefit from the enactment of this program?
   e. What are the strengths of the program?
   f. What weaknesses are critics likely to identify about the program? How can these concerns be addressed?
   g. Who are likely to be allies in supporting funding for this program?
   h. Are there likely to be any groups opposed to fnding this program?

26. Discussion Question: The text identifies a central question with which we must grapple if we are to successfully address the housing shortage in the United States. "How do we provide housing for the poor in a society that values housing for profit, when the poor, on their own, do not possess the resources to ensure a profit for the owners of this housing?" What thoughts and ideas do you have about this important issue?

   Answer: We can give money to the poor or to landlords. This subsidy makes up the difference between the amount a landlord needs to profit and what the poor can pay. Alternatively, we can turn some housing into a cooperatively run community trust. Families live in this housing, but cannot sell it for profit when they leave. Commonly used in other countries, this policy trades off the possibility of making a lot of money in the real estate market for the assurance of safe, affordable community.

Using the Policy Analysis Model

The questions that follow are proposed simply as a guide to help students analyze housing programs and policies from the perspective of the model's five conceptual areas: economics, politics, ideology, social movements, and history.

27. When we look at housing programs through the lens of economics, what do we learn? What economic functions do housing programs and policies serve?

28. When we look at housing programs through the lens of politics, what do we learn? What political functions do housing programs and policies serve? What political issues are embedded in housing policies?

29. When we look at housing programs through the lens of ideology, what do we learn? What are the ideological underpinnings of housing policies and programs? Who benefits from the reinforcement of these ideological ideals?

30. When we look at housing programs through the lens of social movements, what do we learn? What role have social movements played in the development of housing programs and policies?

31. When we look at housing programs through the lens of history, what do we learn? What has been our historical experience with regard to the development of housing programs? Have there been particular "historical moments" that provided the right context for the development of these programs? Have there been different historical stages that mark the development of housing programs?

Chapter 11

Health Care: Programs and Policies

Summary: In U.S. public policy, few issues generate more intense feelings than health care. Rising health care costs, ever increasing insurance premiums, and the growing number of people unable to afford health care coverage have made this one of America's most pressing public policy issues. The material in this chapter is designed to acquaint students with the key policy issues underlying the ongoing debate about how best to meet the health care needs of the American people. In addition, Blau demonstrates how health care policy can be more easily understood through the application of the policy model.

Key Concepts: managed care, HMO, PPO, POS, rationing of care, Medicare, Medicaid, State Children's Health Insurance Plan, DRG, universal health care, single-payer system, mental health parity, national health service

Test Bank: The following questions have been designed to highlight the key concepts and ideas covered in this chapter. They may be used to test students' understanding of the material or to lead class discussions.

1. As an American, you may be angry at our health care system for all of the following reasons EXCEPT
    a. HMOs may block your access to treatment you consider necessary.
    b. You may not be able to afford health insurance.
    c. * American medical technology is not very advanced
    d. Health care is not rationed equitably among all citizens.

2. Health care is often rationed by
    a. limiting health care facilities.
    b. controlling and limiting referrals to specialists.
    c. relying on social policy to determine what type of medical services are most needed and funding these services with large amounts of money.
    d. * all of the above.

3. All of the following are features of our market-based system of health care EXCEPT
    a. services are rationed primarily by price.
    b. most individuals receive their health insurance from their employer.
    c. we have a two-tiered system of health care.
    d. * the U.S. system of health care is among the least costly of all industrialized nations.

4. Discussion Question: What factors contribute to the high cost of health care in the United States? How do you think high health care costs could be contained? How would you balance the issue of health care cost containment with the issue of adequate health care services for all?

Answer: The factors contributing to the high cost of health care in the United States include the cost of drugs, medical technology, and a complex, profit-oriented private sector bureaucracy.

5. Discussion Question: Do you think the United States should have a system of universal health care coverage? What are the arguments you would make in favor of a universal system of health care? What arguments would you make against a universal system of health care?

   Answer: The arguments for a universal system of health care are that
   a. universal health care is a right: with one-seventh of the population lacking health insurance, universal health care would be more humane.
   b. those without access to health care have poorer health outcomes.
   c. we often pay for the health care of the uninsured anyway, in expensive settings like emergency rooms when the treatment has been delayed, and the condition has become more serious.
   d. comprehensive national reform is the only way to rationalize an unwieldy private sector bureaucracy.
   e. if rationing is necessary, it should be done democratically as part of a national dialogue.

   The arguments against a universal system of health care are that
   a. it will be expensive.
   b. it will require a large federal bureaucracy.
   c. it will erode the doctor-patient relationship.

6. Critics of the high cost of the U.S. system of health care cite all of the following EXCEPT
   a. the comparatively high rate of infant mortality in the United States.
   b. the low life expectancy rate of Americans compared with other nations.
   c. * the rising cost of medical services due to the large number of people demanding alternative and complementary medical techniques.
   d. the wastefulness and inefficiency of the overall health care system.

7. T/F*: The U.S. system of health care emphasizes disease *prevention* rather than the *treatment* of disease.

8. Discussion Question: Discuss the influences of urbanization and industrialization on the development of public policy as it relates to health care.

   Answer: As the country industrialized and urban areas grew, the possibility of public health hazards greatly increased. Everyone began to realize that if an epidemic began, none would be completely safe. Therefore, public policy began to focus on health care issues and the development of policies to prevent the spread of disease.

9. Historically, the development of public policy related to health care was connected to all of the following EXCEPT
    a. urbanization and industrialization leading to widespread epidemics
    b. the burden placed on existing health care services by the poor with young children
    c. * the threat of nuclear war during the cold war years.
    d. the need to maintain a healthy labor force.

10. T/F*: Humanitarian concerns were the primary reason policymakers in the nineteenth century became interested in health care issues.

11. Policymakers' interest in health care issues has resulted in
    a. the enactment of Medicaid and Medicare to provide health care coverage for the poor, the chronically ill, and the retired.
    b. efforts at cost-containment such as DRGs, HMOs, and managed care.
    c. sharply improved health outcomes for all Americans.
    d. * a and b only.

12. T*/F: The goal of managed care is to balance the need for cost containment with the provision of quality services

13. All of the following are types of managed care plans EXCEPT
    a. * GPOs.
    b. PPOs.
    c. HMOs.
    d. POSs.

14. The type of managed care plan where a primary care physician controls access to the network of providers is known as
    a. PPO.
    b. * POS.
    c. WTO.
    d. None of the above.

15. A fee-for-service health care program means
    a. an employer pays one annual fee and all employees are covered for all health care needs
    b. an individual pays one annual fee and all his/her health care costs are covered.
    c. * individuals only pay for those health care services that they actually use.
    d. none of the above.

16. T*/F: Medicare and Medicaid are fee-for-service programs.

17. T*/F: Fee-for -service health care plans create an incentive for doctors to offer patients as

many health care services as possible.

18. T/F*: Fee-for-service health care plans have been a way to control rapidly rising health care costs.

19. T/F*: Health maintenance organizations (HMOs) and managed care have proved to be an effective way of controlling rising health care costs.

20. T*/F: The primary publicly funded health care programs are Medicaid, Medicare, and the Children's Health Insurance Plan (CHIPS).

21. T*/F: Under a managed care system of health care, insurers try to balance the need for cost containment with access to quality health care services.

22. T*/F: HMOs are prepaid managed care networks that guarantee patients a range of health care services for a fixed monthly fee.

23. T*/F: Supporters of HMOs argue that they have an incentive to keep patients healthy to keep costs down.

24. Critics of a managed care system of health care delivery make all of the following arguments EXCEPT
    a. It has diverted health care policy-makers from exploring better systems of health care delivery.
    b. It may not have lowered health care costs when administrative costs are factored in.
    c. *It has stymied important medical research efforts directed toward finding cures for Alzheimer's disease, AIDS, and certain cancers.
    d. It does nothing to address the issue of the large number of individuals without health care coverage.

25. Discussion Question: Blau states that the key question about managed care is whether it is rationing care for logical or self-interested motives. What do you think? What has been the experience of the clients with whom you work in accessing needed health care? What has been the experience of clients with regard to accessing quality health care?

26. Discussion Question: The CEO of the Kaiser Health Plan has expressed the view that trying to use financial tools to change the delivery of health care doesn't work and makes people mad. Blau argues that if managed care cannot solve the problems of the health care system, people will get mad and will fight back. What is your view of these arguments? Have we seen any examples of people "fighting back" against the managed care system?

27. T*/F: Medicaid is a federal/state program that provides medical assistance to low-income people.

28. All of the following are eligible for Medicaid EXCEPT
    a. low-income families with dependent children.
    b. low-income elderly people.
    c. blind and disabled individuals.
    d. *anyone who has worked at least 10 years and has had Social Security deducted from his/her paycheck.

29. T/F*: Medicaid coverage and benefits are identical in each state.

30. T*/F: The federal government does require that certain medical services must be a part of every state's Medicaid program.

31. T*/F: The rate of reimbursement paid by the federal government for Medicaid services is greater in poorer states than the rate paid in wealthier states.

32. T/F*: In any given year, the percentage of poor people receiving Medicaid benefits is close to 100 percent.

33. T*/F: The 1996 welfare reform act disconnected Medicaid benefits from public assistance benefits.

34. T*/F: Since the welfare reform act of 1996, a large number of Medicaid recipients have been enrolled in managed care programs.

35. Critics of the practice of enrolling Medicaid recipients in managed care plans cite all of the following EXCEPT
    a. * Medicaid managed care encourages participants to use more medical services than necessary.
    b. Managed care companies have little experience working with high-risk, multiproblem, inner-city clients.
    c. Managed care regulations assume that an individual will have access to a telephone and the ability to access the information necessary to make prudent medical decisions.
    d. Managed care companies have little experience providing the type of supportive services such as outreach and case management required by many Medicaid recipients.

36. All of the following statements are TRUE about Medicaid EXCEPT
    a. One of the largest single costs for the Medicaid program is covering expenses associated with individuals needing long-term care.
    b. Medicaid functions as an important back-up source of health care services for the poor elderly who also receive Medicare.

  c. * Children of immigrants who receive Medicaid benefits disqualify their parents from eligibility for citizenship.

  d. 68 percent of nursing home residents are dependent upon Medicaid to cover part of their long-term care costs.

37. All of the following are TRUE about Medicare EXCEPT

  a. * Chances are that the health care costs of an individual receiving Medicare will be covered 100 percent by the Medicare program.

  b. As of 2003, the Medicare program does not cover the costs of medical necessities such as prescription drugs, dental work, hearing aids, and eyeglasses.

  c. Medicare is a national insurance program for the elderly.

  d. Medicare is financed through a payroll tax that is part of Social Security.

38. Which of the following is TRUE about the Medicare program?

  a. * Most beneficiaries of Medicare must pay out of their own pocket for supplemental insurance to cover the gaps in Medicare coverage.

  b. Most eligible seniors do not elect to receive Medicare benefits.

  c. There is a stigma attached to receiving Medicare benefits much like that attached to receiving Medicaid benefits.

  d. The federal government opposes making HMOs part of the Medicare system.

39. Which of the following is a TRUE statement?

  a. The federal government does not allocate any funds to cover uninsured children.

  b. * Children in families with income equal to 200 percent of the federal poverty level are eligible for government- funded health insurance.

  c. Most states have increased property taxes to pay for a health insurance program for poor children.

  d. None of the above.

40. All of the following are true statements EXCEPT

  a. * Judging by the number of children enrolled and the expenditure of available funds, the State Children's Health Insurance Plan has been a big success.

  b. Many states participating in the State Children's Health Insurance Plan did not enroll enough children to use up all of the allocated federal money.

  c. Most health policy experts agree that the State Children's Health Insurance Plan has not adequately addressed the problem of uninsured children.

  d. Some states did not use their allocated federal funds to provide benefits under the State Children's Health Insurance Plan because they were unwilling to contribute matching funds.

41. Blau identifies all of the following as problems related to health care in the United States EXCEPT

  a. the large number of people who are uninsured.

    b. * overuse of the health care system.

    c. the lack of prescription drug coverage for many people.

    d. the lack of parity for mental health policy.

42. T*/F: Men and women with low income are much more likely to die of certain chronic aliments and communicable diseases than men and women with higher income.

43. T/F*: Research has proven that race is not a factor in receiving adequate health care in the United States.

44. All of the following are TRUE statements EXCEPT

    a. Minorities receive poorer medical treatment than whites.

    b. Some insurance companies limit access to medical services more strictly for minorities than for whites.

    c. * Doctors tend to believe that whites will be less likely than people of color to participate in follow-up medical care.

    d. Whites tend to have longer relationships with their doctors than do minorities.

45. Discussion Question: Blau draws on health policy literature and research to make the point that inequality kills irrespective of the riskier health behaviors in which some poor people engage. What points does he cite to support this argument? Do these arguments hold true for your clients? Give some examples from your practice.

    Answer: Blau makes the following points:

    a. People who are poor are less likely to see a doctor for a health care need than those with higher incomes.

    b. Because poor people don't have the money to access needed health care services, simple medical problems often end up as much more serious or complicated problems that may require hospitalization.

    c. Because the affluent do have access to good health care, they are often reluctant to support health care services for the poor such as public hospitals and low-cost/no-cost clinics.

    d. The stresses of survival for those at or below the poverty level often prevent them from developing social networks that support people in times of trouble and help to keep people alive.

46. Discussion Question: In what ways does the health care policy of the United States either reflect or reject the principle argued by Blau that inequality kills?

    Answer: Women with incomes under $10,000 a year are more than three times as likely to die of heart disease, and nearly three times as likely to die of diabetes, as those with incomes above $25,000. Men with less than a high school education are more than twice as likely to die of heart disease, and nearly twice as likely to die of communicable diseases, as those with more than thirteen years of schooling.

47. T*/F: In 2002, the number of Americans without health insurance was approximately 14 percent.

48. Blau argues that the most flagrant deficiency of the U.S. system of health care is
    a. overuse of the system by poor people.
    b. * the large number of people without health insurance coverage.
    c. the lack of interest by the medical profession in alternative forms of health care.
    d. the lack of proper sanitary conditions in hospitals.

49. T*/F: Blau argues that there are invisible but significant costs involved in having a large percentage of the population without health insurance coverage.

50. Which of the following are costs associated with having a large percentage of the population without health care coverage?
    a. a lower literacy rate.
    b. * lost worker productivity and excessive emergency room costs.
    c. workers retiring at an earlier age.
    d. lower wages for doctors.

51. T/F*: The majority of the people without health care coverage are from families living below the poverty line.

52. T*/F: One factor influencing the growing percentage of people without health insurance coverage is that many workers lose their health benefits when they lose their jobs.

53. T/F*: The welfare reform act of 1996 greatly expanded health care benefits to immigrants.

54. The group most likely to lack health care benefits in the United States is:
    a. African Americans.
    b. Asians.
    c. * Latinos.
    d. lesbians and gay men.

55. Many immigrants to this country do not have health benefits because
    a. the premiums are too high given their low salaries.
    b. they work for employers who do not offer health care benefits.
    c. their low salaries exclude them from the health care coverage offered to other employees.
    d. * all of the above.

56. T*/F: Mothers constitute another significant group of uninsured Americans.

57. All of the following are ramifications of mothers lacking health care coverage EXCEPT
    a. * preventing successful breastfeeding of their newborns.
    b. putting them at greater risk for serious health problems.
    c. endangering their capacity to care for their children.
    d. endangering the health of any babies they might have in the future.

58. People without health care coverage are likely to do all of the following EXCEPT
    a. not fill a prescription because of its cost.
    b. skip preventive health care services.
    c. * sue their doctor for malpractice.
    d. not see a doctor when they need one.

59. T/F*: Older Americans covered by Medicare are able to have prescription medications paid for by the program.

60. T*/F: Prescription drug costs are the fastest growing part of health care expenses.

61. Drug companies argue that the high costs of their products are justified by:
    a. the high rate at which they are taxed by the federal government.
    b. * the high cost of drug research.
    c. the high cost of advertising and marketing drugs.
    d. the high cost of their contributions to political action committees and individual political campaigns.

62. T*/F: Critics of pharmaceutical companies' drug pricing policies point to the relatively small percentage of money spent by these companies on drug research and development.

63. T*/F: Drug companies have been known to pay competitors to keep cheaper generic drugs off the market.

64. Discussion Question: The problem of rapidly escalating drug costs is one of the most pressing issues of the American health care system. To begin to address this problem, what are some of the questions policymakers must consider?

    Answer:
    a. Who should be covered by a prescription drug benefit? Everyone? Only the elderly? Children?
    b. How generous should a prescription drug benefit be? How much of the cost should be covered?
    c. How should a prescription drug benefit be financed? Through tax incentives for drug manufacturers? Through block grant funding? Through income tax deductions? Other?

65. Discussion Question: Blau notes that much drug research actually begins with public funding (grant money, etc.), and pharmaceutical companies build on this research to create drugs that earn them billions of dollars. Do you believe the public should accrue some benefit from the sale of drugs whose funding originates in the public sector? What type of system could we develop to reduce the price of these drugs?

    Answer: The National Institute of Health could increase competition by developing drugs on its own. Alternatively, the government could set stricter pricing rules for drugs developed with public money. We could also speed up the process of drugs becoming generic.

66. Which of the following is a TRUE statement about mental health care in the United States?
    a. All insurance companies that cover physical health care needs must offer equal coverage for mental health needs.
    b. President Ronald Reagan took steps to enact a national mental health policy.
    c. Managed care companies have lobbied Congress to be able to expand the number of mental health services they can offer.
    d. * Health care policy in this country has never recognized mental health needs as equally important or worthy of funding as physical health needs.

67. T*/F: Almost every developed country other than the United States has a system of national health care.

68. Which of the following is a TRUE statement?
    a. The terms "national health service" and "national health insurance" mean the same thing.
    b. * In a national health service, the government pays the salaries of the doctors, nurses, and other medical personnel.
    c. With national health insurance, all health personnel become government employees.
    d. Countries that have a national health service charge patients a fee equal to the going market rate.

69. Under the Canadian single-payer model of health care
    a. individuals secure their own private health insurance and are reimbursed by the government.
    b. * the government negotiates with the health care system and serves as the sole insurer.
    c. the government "nationalizes" all health care services, making them all "public" as opposed to private services.
    d. one company is designated by the government as the sole provider of health care insurance in exchange for agreeing to accept lower insurance premiums.

70. Which is a TRUE statement about the Canadian health care system today?
    a. The Canadian system covers the cost of drugs.
    b. The cost of administering the Canadian program is far greater than the cost of health

care administration in the United States.
    c. The Canadian system covers the cost of dentistry and eye care.
    d. * The Canadian system has had to adopt stricter rationing of health care to respond to rising costs.

71. One obstacle to enacting a single-payer health care system in the United States is
    a. there is no interest in this type of health care system.
    b. insurance premiums would rise.
    c. * taxes would have to be increased to pay for this type of program.
    d. all of the above.

72. Discussion Question: Blau argues that the values underlying the American economic system stand in contradiction to the values underlying the U.S. health care system. Do you agree with him? Why or why not? Give some examples from your fieldwork internship.

    Answer: Competition does not work in health care because patients do not shop for health care procedures based on price. And although many people value the profit motive in other enterprises, they recoil at the prospect that people might make money in health care at the cost of lives.

73. Blau argues that the major reason for our excessive health care spending is
    a. overuse of the system by people who cannot pay.
    b. cost inflation caused by the big run-up in the stock market during the 1990's.
    c. not enough hospital beds for all who need them.
    d. * the excessive profit and waste that is built into the American health care system.

74. Discussion Question: Blau argues that the huge amount of money spent by drug companies and other interest groups on campaign contributions, lobbying, and issue ads is a big factor in keeping our health care system bloated and wasteful and has led to a "policy paralysis." According to his analysis, how does this process work? Do you think there should be limits on the amount of money drug companies and other health care interest groups can spend on lobbying legislators? Defend your position.

    Answer: As one of the largest lobbying groups, the health care industry spends huge sums of money to ensure that relevant legislation does not violate its interests. Since some critics attribute the major problems of the health care system—the number of uninsured, high drug costs, and wasteful administrative practices—to these same interests, they criticize the health care industry for perpetuating a policy paralysis that blocks real reform. Ceilings on campaign spending might help to end this political paralysis, but they do not really work, because contributors will always find the loopholes. In the interim, a better solution—public financing of election campaigns—has barely surfaced on the political agenda.

75. The American ideology linking work and health insurance
    a. assumes that everyone has a job.
    b. acts as a major impediment to the development of a national health care system.
    c. does not take into account that many low-paid jobs do not offer health insurance.
    d. * all of the above.

76. Discussion Question: Blau argues that because health care has been treated as a commodity like other consumer goods, many Americans believe it should be purchased on the open market. What are the implications of this belief?

    Answer: This belief leads to the health care system we now have—one that is costly, inefficient, and whose health care outcomes closely reflect income inequalities.

77. T*/F: Blau argues that Americans' fear of a strong federal government has been a major factor in defeating any plan for a national health care system.

78. T*/F: After the defeat of President Clinton's 1994 health care bill, many advocates for universal health coverage have turned their lobbying efforts to individual states.

79. T/F*: The first major presidential candidate to endorse the concept of national health insurance was Lyndon B. Johnson

80. Historically, all of the following have derailed any efforts at implementing universal health care coverage in the United States EXCEPT
    a. fear of increased taxes.
    b. * fear of creating competition among health care providers.
    c. fear of creating a large federal bureaucracy.
    d. fear of losing the ability to choose one's health care providers.

Using the Policy Analysis Model

The questions that follow are proposed simply as a guide to help students analyze health care programs and policies from the perspective of the model's five conceptual areas: economics, politics, ideology, social movements, and history.

81. When we look at health care programs through the lens of economics, what do we learn? What economic functions do health care programs and policies serve?

82. When we look at health care programs through the lens of politics, what do we learn? What political functions do health care programs and policies serve? What political issues are embedded in health care policies?

83. When we look at health care programs through the lens of ideology, what do we learn?

What are the ideological underpinnings of health care policies and programs? Who benefits from the reinforcement of these ideological ideals?

84. When we look at health care programs through the lens of social movements, what do we learn? What role have social movements played in the development of health care programs and policies?

85. When we look at health care programs through the lens of history, what do we learn? What has been our historical experience with regard to the development of health care programs? Have there been particular "historical moments" that provided the right context for the development of these programs? Have there been different historical stages that mark the development of health care programs?

Chapter 12

Food and Hunger: Programs and Policies

Summary: This chapter highlights a social problem in the United States that, on some levels, defies explanation: how, in a country where food is plentiful and cheap, can hunger be a problem? How, in a land of extraordinary abundance, can people go hungry? This chapter lays out the dimensions of the problem of hunger in the United States, as well as its effects on physical and psychological health. It describes the different food entitlement programs and proposes a system of classification to help students identify the differences and similarities among them. The author also helps students to understand some of the factors that set hunger apart from other social problems. He then explores whether these differences in the perception of hunger have led to the growth of a charitable food network that actually undermines the goal of feeding the poor.

The conclusion of the chapter offers students the opportunity to see how the application of the policy analysis model described in this text can be used to analyze the problem of hunger. In this process, the application of this model can help them to reach a more informed decision about where they stand in the debate over entitlements versus charity.

Key Concepts: hunger, potential hunger, food security, food insecurity, malnutrition, social costs, food stamps, WIC Program, National School Lunch Program, School Breakfast Program, Summer Food Service Program for Children, Child and Adult Care Food Program, Emergency Food Assistance Program, the private food assistance network, Second Harvest

Test Bank: The following questions have been designed to highlight the key concepts and ideas covered in this chapter. They may be used to test students' understanding of the material or to lead class discussions.

1. Discussion Question: The author argues that hunger is different from other social problems. What does he mean?

   Answer: The author makes the case that hunger, unlike certain other social problems (for example, drug use), has no "payoff" or pleasure. Therefore, it is a problem that is less likely to be seen as a personal fault of the sufferer. Consequently, the general public is able to mobilize around this issue in ways that are not evident when we look at the public's response to other social problems and issues.

2. The circumstance in which someone cannot obtain enough food, even if the condition does not lead to a health problem, is the definition of
   a. food security.
   b. food insecurity.
   c. malnutrition.
   d. * potential hunger.

3. According to the best available research, what percentage of American households faces

some degree of "food insecurity"?
    a. 1 percent.
    b. *10 percent
    c. 25 percent
    d. 45 percent

4. Forty percent of the people who live in food-insecure households are
    a. * children.
    b. pregnant mothers.
    c. single mothers.
    d. the elderly.

5. Within the low-income population, all of the following groups are at high risk for hunger and food insecurity EXCEPT
    a. Mexican Americans
    b. families without health insurance.
    c. * young African American men.
    d. families whose head of household has not completed high school.

6. Women represent a disproportionate share of those who receive emergency food aid because
    a. they are less educated than men.
    b. they are more apt to go to food pantries and soup kitchens than are men.
    c. * the provisions of welfare reform affected them more severely.
    d. they are not good at budgeting.

7. Discussion Question: Why should the fact that some people don't get enough to eat matter as an issue of social policy?

Answer: Although some might argue that addressing hunger should not be a social policy concern, most would argue that a lack of adequate food affects one's health, ability to learn, and productivity. In addition, not having enough to eat, like not being able to provide for any basic need, fosters feelings of inadequacy and worthlessness. These are the social costs of hunger.

8. All of the following have triggered changes in how we address the issues of hunger and food insufficiency EXCEPT
    a. social movements designed to make the issue more visible.
    b. farm overproduction and the power of agricultural interests.
    c. a decline in government-sponsored food entitlement programs leading to a rise in the number of private charities stepping in to address the need.
    d. *a lawsuit forcing the government to change its policies.

9. T*/F: According to the 2001 U.S. Conference of Mayors' annual survey, requests for emergency food assistance have risen by almost 23 percent

10. T/F*: The lack of a job, by itself, is enough to explain why some individuals do not have sufficient food.

11. Class Exercise: Because the author describes a large number of programs designed to address the issues of hunger and food insufficiency, students may have difficulty grasping the differences among the various programs. An exercise that may prove helpful is to divide the class into several groups and have each group work together to answer the following questions about each food program:
   a. *Who (which sector) provides* the entitlement (e.g., the public sector, the private sector, or some combination of both)?
   b. *What* does the benefit consist of (e.g., cash, food, voucher)?
   c. *To whom* does the program provide the benefit (e.g., adults, children, elderly, the poor, the working poor)?
   d. *Who pays* for the benefit (e.g., taxpayers, private charity)?

   Putting the answers to these questions in chart form will provide the students with an easy way to note the similarities and differences among the various programs.

Using the Policy Analysis Model

The following questions are designed to help students analyze programs and policies that address hunger and food insufficiency from the perspective of the model's five conceptual areas: economics, politics, ideology, social movements, and history.

12. When we look at programs designed to address hunger and food insufficiency through the lens of economics, what do we learn? What economic functions do these programs and policies serve?

13. When we look at programs designed to address hunger and food insufficiency through the lens of politics, what do we learn? What political functions do these programs and policies serve? What political issues are embedded in hunger policies?

14. When we look at programs designed to address hunger and food insufficiency through the lens of ideology, what do we learn? What are the ideological underpinnings of policies and programs that address hunger? Who benefits from the reinforcement of these ideological ideals?

15. When we look at programs designed to address hunger and food insufficiency through the lens of social movements, what do we learn? What role have social movements played in the development of hunger programs and policies?

16. When we look at programs designed to address hunger and food insufficiency through the lens of history, what do we learn? What has been our historical experience with regard to the development of programs to address hunger? Have there been particular "historical moments" that provided the right context for the development of these programs? Have there been different historical stages that mark the development of programs to address hunger and food insufficiency?

Chapter 13

Conclusion: If You Want to Analyze a Policy

Summary: In this concluding chapter, the authors summarize the central themes running through the text and challenge students to take on the mantle of social change. Because students should have a much clearer understanding of the link between policy and practice, and because they now have a policy model to draw on, they should feel much better equipped not only to identify social problems, but also to advocate and fight for positive social changes.

1. Discussion Question: Having covered all of the material in this text, would you now agree with the authors that every form of social work practice embodies a social policy? Why or why not? What social policy issues are you seeing in your work with clients? How has learning the material in this text helped you in your work with clients?

2. Discussion Question: One central theme running throughout this text is the premise that because social work practice embodies policy, knowledge about policy is essential to ensure that our practice is conscious and informed. What are your thoughts about this premise?

3. Discussion Question: Another theme running through this text is the notion of social change and how social change comes about. Blau and Abramovitz argue that the greatest advances in the development of social welfare policy have come about because of the active involvement of many people in great social movements. What are some policy areas that you see in your work with clients that could benefit from the formation of a social movement to fight for change?

4. Discussion Question: This chapter contends that knowledge about the influence of economics, politics, ideology, history and social movements on the formation of social policy helps us to understand the often hostile policy environment in which social workers operate. Give some examples from your practice that illustrate this point.